PRISON FATHERS PARENTING BEHIND BARS

Latif M. Bossman

Prison Fathers Parenting Behind Bars

Copyright © 2017 by Latif Bossman.

A paperback origional

First Edition : September 2017

For information contact :

Latif M. Bossman

(503) 660-2321

albossman1855@gmail.com

Book and Cover design by Designer

ISBN 978-1983556036

© Registration TXu 2-046-654

Reviews

Prison Fathers: Parenting Behind Bars is a riveting narrative of one man's experience, that mirrors a desire expressed by countless incarcerated men to connect and have a meaningful relationship with their offspring. As an Islamic Prison Chaplain, I have personally witnessed this narrative unfold. Latif has modeled and is now sharing a blueprint of parenting inside oneself, while inside prison. And it's profound impact on the innocent child.
-Imam Mikal H Shabazz, Director: Oregon Islamic Chaplains Organization.

"Latif Bossman presents a unique and much needed perspective on fatherhood in the context of incarceration. Love, respect and good parenting can survive prison, and he helps men achieve that with his honest story."
- D. Lou Raymond, **Author of Dodging Africa.**

Mr. Bossman's very personal story aimed at educating other prisoners about his methods of maintaining his fathering during his 6-year incarceration is inspiring and heart-breaking but a practical and passionate call to action. His statistics are well researched while he also offers a penetrating view of his painful experience with his children during incarceration. But the main message of his well-written book is to implore others "to be an active father while in prison." He offers methods and skills he used to successfully maintain his relationships with his children. Helping men to father while in prison is a much-needed area of study and reporting. I highly recommend Mr. Bossman's book for those incarcerated, those interested in fighting the epidemic of father absence due in part to incarceration and those interested in inmate's quality of life. I hope he will have the opportunity to educate prisoners through a speaking tour.
-Raymond Levy, PsyD

Latif Bossman has written a practical "how to" parenting book drawing upon his own experience both as the child of an imprisoned father as well as his life as the imprisoned father of his own two children. His "action items" are not only good guidance for those fathers behind bars, but also for those fathers who are not imprisoned. Although written for inmates it's about good parenting behind bars or not.
-Rev. Warren R. Radtke

Prison Fathers: Parenting Behind Bars by Latif Bossman spells out the importance of fathers staying connected with their children during incarceration. The author describes his positive, proactive experience of parenting behind bars. His first published work is a testament to the bonding impact of forgiveness.
-Dr. Mel King, author of Chain of Change: Struggles for Black Community 1st Development

Parenting is difficult enough, now imagine raising a child while you're in prison. More than half of the 2.2 million people incarcerated in the United States are parents. More than 90 percent are men. Latif Bossman was one of them and he's written a how -to-book with practical and powerful ways to parent from behind bars but it has lessons for all of us. Prison reform will have little affect unless we break the inter-generational cycle of violence and crime that comes when a society makes children victims of crime.
-Bruce Gellerman, Senior Correspondent of WBUR Boston

Acknowledgments

To all my editors and the countless hours that were spent to help me bring this memoir to its full potential and convey my experience in a manner that may help fathers who face the challenge of parenting from prison.

Although a challenge, it is still possible to be a productive parent while incarcerated. By using all means at your disposal along with creative ideas you can continue to parent and provide as much love, emotional support and financial support as possible regardless of the bars which have you physically trapped in. I have climbed this mountain and for every incarcerated father, I hope the steps that I took that enabled me to parent successfully while incarcerated can be used as a guide on your journey and that the bond between you and each of your children will be strengthened.

I'd also like to say a word of appreciation to all my teachers, thanks to whom I made it out alive and intact, and moved on to a better life. This blessed group includes the hardened ones and the fiercest in the Department of Corrections in the State of Oregon. They were the Yin to my Yang at a confused time in my own evolution as a human being. My hat goes off to them - my jailers helped polish my diamond.

All praises due to the Creator for giving me the strength to parent through adversity and for giving me the strength to be a better Father

CONTENTS

Foward

I dedicate this book to the fathers across America who have continued to raise and love their children through prison walls, razor wire, and steel bars. Men who have chosen sacrifice over self-pity, who see their future, not for themselves, but for their children. This is for the fathers who are unmoved by the plague of their own misery, hurt, pain, loneliness, and ignorance, but instead are motivated by the love, of their children in truth, hope, forgiveness, and determination to remain an active father, regardless of their situation.

I write to tell your story, my story, of men who struggle to continue to be an active father to their children against the odds, while still incarcerated. Parenting their children in sterile visiting rooms, through letters, or on collect telephone calls, and, when fortunate, they are able to communicate through all these channels, to maintain the bond of father and son and father and daughter. When the odds are stacked against us dads, how do they do it? How did I do it?

Consider a moment that in 2010, 1.5 million people were in State or Federal prison in the U.S, and 750,000 in jails (Rutgers Camden, Children and Families of the Incarcerated, Fact Sheet); 92% of people in prison are male, 8% female (Cited: Glaze, L. Correctional Populations in the U.S. 2010. Bureau of Justice Statistics. Washington, DC. 2011). In 2007, 52% of prisoners were parents. This amounts to 1.1 million absent fathers and 120,000 absent mothers—affecting 2.7 million children—within the prison system alone. Nationally, there are more than 120,000 incarcerated mothers and 1.1 million incarcerated fathers who are parents of minor children (ages 0-17) (Cited: Glaze, L. and Maruschak, L. Parents in Prison and Their Minor Children. Bureau of Justice Statistics, Washington, D.C. 2011). And, 44-55% of fathers had at least one minor child living with them before incarceration (Cited: Ibid.).

What becomes of these children when over 60% of prisoners

are sent to prisons 100 miles away from home?

I wanted to share more information about prison and the apparent default setting in a very broken system that all too often entraps and imprisons.

Or, how, due to color of skin or ethnicity many are sentenced unfairly.

Or, how the head food coordinator for the state of Oregon prisons was arrested and indicted for taking kickbacks from vendors to buy food whose shelf-life had long expired (he got caught during the fifth year of my sentence.).

Or, how one day a guard at the minimum facility, from which I was released, told me the eggs they served for breakfast were not fit for human consumption, and he himself didn't eat any food served at the prison.

The point I am trying to make is that—though my source material abounds—I don't want to stray from the focus of this book, being an active father while in prison. Really, breaking down the matrix of the potential for improvement within the prison system from a technical standpoint, assessed through the eyes of a former inmate, would end up being another book entirely.

My purpose here is to share the importance of men and the importance of men to uphold their parenting responsibility regardless of incarceration. The toll on the family and particularly the child is well documented. Children of incarcerated parents, suffer from anxiety, depression and acting out. And it is three-fold when they lose contact with their father. This book is intended to encourage and give the how-to for incarcerated men to continue their parenting.

A father's imprisonment does not negate his responsibility to parent. Yes, imprisonment takes away your freedom, and your family feels the pain of you not being there with them; they are impacted by the void created by your absence. Yet your love and dreams for your children can and must remain in your heart and mind to mobilize you to consistent action.

There is no time for self-pity. The child is the victim, not having the father available; therefore, it is the father's responsibility to reduce the child's stress from the separation by explaining the situation as honestly as possible, and communicating effectively according to the child's age. And if the father can explain, with the child present in the visiting room, with the other parent present, that would be the ideal situation.

Before you tell the child the details of your circumstances, always make sure the other parent agrees with the plan to share it with the child. Incarcerated fathers must make their presence and love felt through the prison walls and project it into the minds and hearts of their children. These fathers must take advantage of every opportunity given to reach this goal. By doing this a father will never be forgotten by his children. And when visiting hours are over, his children will continue to miss him and question why Dad cannot come home with them. Or, they will wonder why they can't call you whenever they want to.

For those fortunate individuals who have never had to experience imprisonment, my hope is that you gain insight and understanding into the world and the challenges of incarcerated fathers and the struggles they face in continuing to parent while incarcerated.

Introduction

My name is Latif Bossman and I was an inmate in the Department of Corrections in the State of Oregon. On October 31, 2001, I was sentenced to five years and ten months for four counts of second degree robbery. At the time of conviction, I was twenty-five-years-old, and was the father of a three-and-a-half-year-old son.

Aside from living and breathing, the relationship between my son Hakeem and I was truthfully the best feeling on earth. My son was born on November 10, 1997, and I was present at his birth. As I witnessed his entrance into the world, I knew I was the luckiest man alive. From that day forward, I vowed never to abandon him, no matter the circumstances, because I wanted his reality to be different from what I had experienced growing up.

At the age of four, I, like many kids in my neighborhood, became the product of a broken home. But unlike many children of divorced parents, my father remained present in my life. Many thanks go to my mother who kept the lines of communication open, and made sure—no matter what—that my father was able to maintain a relationship with my sister and me. I think the most important thing after a divorce is for children to know that their parent is accessible, available and one hundred percent committed to raising them. Regardless of who has custody, a child must always be able to have a direct-line of communication, regular contact and interaction with the non-custodial parent.

My father had been elated when he learned that my mother was expecting. He was present at my birth also, cut my umbilical cord, and named me Latif. Even with this solid foundation and his intention to be a good parent, my experience with my father is not what I had hoped for. However, in spite of my feelings about our relationship, it was critical to me that he never denied me. He made himself available and tried to stay in contact with me and provided financial support to help make sure that my daily needs were met. He always made sure that I knew where he lived and how to reach him. And he had an open-door policy for me.

On a regular basis, he made sure that I could spend the night at his house, and always had food for me to eat. I loved the fact I could be with my Dad. He always encouraged me to just hang out with him and talk. And cook. These were major grounding points between us that kept me connected to him. As a young boy and as a young man, I needed that. He made sure to create special times for my sister Starr and me, giving each of us equal amounts of attention. He shared his life with us, and the importance of honesty, education, and the importance of having a strong work ethic.

My father was a hard worker and always had a job until he was laid off. He replaced employment with volunteer work, coordinating a community garden and mentoring youth at our local community center. My father showed his love by providing home-cooked meals for my sister and me, and he was a great cook. He knew nutrition was essential for the healthy development of children, and he practiced it by feeding us correctly with healthy foods and a balanced diet.

And I have continued that tradition by cooking home meals for my children. My Dad shared his wisdom with parables, and his most memorable was, "Where we come from is a long way." As a child, this encouraged me to always look ahead, remember our progress, but never forget where we came from.

A few years after the divorce, my Dad had to make a painful decision, relocating to find work. He had been laid off for about six months and moving was his last option. After he moved out of state, he continued to stay in contact with me through phone calls and letters. I called him often, but it didn't help. I missed him, and I wanted to be with him. So my mother —after discussing it with my father—decided to let me go live with him. I was ten-years-old at the time and was so excited to be leaving my birth state to join my father.

A few weeks after I moved in with my father, I learned he had a drinking problem. Finding him passed out on the couch and stumbling around often were the tell-tale signs I picked up on. My mother was unaware of this when she sent me to live with him and I had no intention of telling her.

In contrast, for more than half of Hakeem's young life, I had been incarcerated. My son was only three-and-a-half when I was incarcerated, and I wasn't released until he was nine-and-a-half-years-old. So, I had more experience as an incarcerated father than as a free father. This is my experience and perspective as a man who chose to be an active father behind prison walls. Every incarcerated father's experience is different, but for those who remain active in their children's lives, have experienced a great number of similarities.

Here are some of the common questions that fathers will hear from their children, at least once during their incarceration: How come you're not here? When will I see you? Why are you in prison? Did you do a bad thing? Are you mad at me? When can I come visit you? And: Where are you?

Chapter One
Where Is My Dad?

WHERE IS MY DAD? Every child asks this at least once when
contact with a parent is lost. The child of an incarcerated parent is
no different. This statement, "Where is my Dad?" is profound and
powerful. I believe it echoes a child's need to feel and rely on the
love and strength a father provides and the comfort and protection
the child feels in his presence. In our society the single-parent home
is more common than not, with 35% of mothers in the U.S. being
the sole provider. (according to The Annie E. Casey Foundation,

National Kids Count program 2011).

So, where are all the fathers? Some are in prison, others enslaved by drugs and alcohol, or, in the worst case, deceased. According to the Bureau of justice Statistics, in 2007 an estimated 744,200 state and federal prisoners in the United States were fathers to 1,599,200 children under the age of 18 (Glaze & Maruschak). And of those, how many maintain a relationship with their children during incarceration?

These questions are posed to open the minds and eyes of the public to a growing epidemic, one that not only affects the current generation, but also future generations of boys and girls who will be influenced by the actions that fathers make today.

First let me say, while I have had a lot of time to think, I am neither in the category of great thinkers, nor am I a doctor, of any sort. I hold no degrees. My knowledge comes from my direct experience as an incarcerated father and the relationship I have had with my son, which manifested during my prison sentence.

On June 24, 2001, I was arrested and charged with three counts of robbery in the first degree and six counts of robbery in the second degree. It was a Wednesday and I was two days away from picking up my son for our weekend together. All week, I looked forward to his happy and energetic personality and the sound of him calling my name, "Dad!"—his voice deep and warm for a little guy—and then he'd leap on me as soon as I got close enough. As I sat in my holding cell, all I could think about was the disappointment my son would feel if I wasn't there to pick him up for our weekend time together.

Well, I ended up disappointing him because I was never released, not until 70 months later. Thus began our relationship through prison walls, collect phone calls, visiting rooms, and written correspondence. A week went by after my arrest before I saw Hakeem, but this time we were separated by three-inch thick glass—obscured by hand prints from past loved ones of other prisoners. My mother brought Hakeem to visit me. As I looked into the big, round, chocolate eyes of my three-and-a-half-year-old son, I saw joy and confusion. I put my hand to the glass and he did the same. My mother gently put the phone to his ear, and the first thing I said, was, "I miss you." He responded by saying, "Daddy how come you didn't come and get me?"

I looked into my son's eyes and didn't know how to answer his question. All I remember saying was, "I am sorry." We talked for a while and I answered a barrage of my son's why's. I don't know what it is, but it seems like kids between age three and five love to ask why about every statement you make to them. Our visit ended with "I love you." I longed to hold my son's hand and walk right out with him. This new vibe I felt stung so deep; I knew things would never be the same again.

For the next two months, the visits between my son and me just got worse. We didn't talk much, and he cried a lot. I think he felt that I had left him. At such a young age, how could my son think otherwise? Even an older child would feel abandoned. My worst fear was materializing: My son thinking that I didn't love him, that I had abandoned him, that I didn't want him anymore.

My second fear was facing the reality that I might not be able to continue my relationship with him, and worst of all that he would forget me. My only hope to re-unite with my son was to beat my case. Then, I could resume our normal relationship and quickly heal the fracture that occurred as a result of our separation.

For the next two months, while I awaited trial, I stressed over how I could make sure that my son did not forget me. Besides the outcome of my case, this was all I thought about. Though I wanted my freedom, I realized that being in prison wasn't my biggest fear. My biggest fear was not being able to contribute to Hakeem's development and not being an integral part of his life.

These thoughts plagued my waking hours, and caused me to toss and turn at night with nightmares of the worst-case scenario, me losing my case. My mind stayed occupied with the questions: What if I lose my case what would happen to my son? What would happen to our relationship? After my personal service to my God, my most urgent priority was—and still is!—that I live to be an active father to my son!

Nonetheless, the nightmare became reality when I was found guilty on four of my nine counts of robbery. The minimum sentence would be seventy months if they were run concurrently and 210 months if they were run consecutively (concurrent meaning together, consecutive meaning one after the other). I was outraged by the outcome of my case, and once again my thoughts raced to how my son would react to my incarceration. I began to think, and wonder how people parent from behind the walls of prison. I asked myself: Can a father parent while incarcerated?

I wondered how it could be possible to be an active father while incarcerated. What could I do to ensure that my son knew that I loved him, and that my being gone was not his fault? I've heard that children often blame themselves when parents' divorce, die, or abandon them. Maybe it's the only way a child can feel like s/he has any control over an out-of-control situation, taking on the burden of blame. All I could think of was how to make sure that my son didn't blame himself for me not being there.

Let me rewind my history here and tell you about my father and our relationship. My father was born in Ghana West Africa. He arrived in Boston, Massachusetts in 1972. He came on a student visa to further his education by attending college in Worcester, MA. There, he met my mother at a college social event where she was looking very striking in a traditional African-style dress and gold earrings that tinkled, casting an air of royalty and magic around her.

She smelled of frankincense, my dad recalled. They married three months later.

My father came from a large family, the oldest of 15 siblings, and the other 14 were all girls. So I was raised with a sense of family, responsibility, and love. Unlike America, Africa doesn't have the single parent epidemic due to non-marital relationships. In the African American culture, single parenting dates back to the enslavement experience, when parents were sold away from their spouses and offspring and vice versa.

Slave owners learned in 1712 from a speech "The Making of a Slave" delivered by Willie Lynch in Virginia that, to make a slave, you must disconnect the male from the home. By taking the father away from his family, it made it easier to break his spirit and control the women and children. So, generation after generation—until the 1965 Reconstruction period—single parent homes became the norm, with the mother most often being the only parent. This is not to say that African Americans don't remain married; they do, of course, and happily. Yet single parenting became a epidemic in the United States for many African American families.

After four-years of marriage, my father and mother divorced. And though my parents themselves had grown up in a unified two-parent home, they still chose divorce. While they remained cordial after their divorce, it was still a painful journey for me. The separation followed by the divorce began the long road of being raised in the aftermath of family dissolution. This was dramatic enough, but then my father quietly and slowly became an alcoholic. I stayed with my father on the weekends and we'd do things together. But gradually over time our outings and activities diminished. Two years after their divorce, he relocated from Boston to Texas. It was then I began to act out.

My mother remarried; I hated her new husband, mainly because he was abusive and mean. During this time, my Mom would call my Dad for me, and we would talk about me moving to Texas. These conversations really helped me—just hearing his voice. He ended every call with, "I love you" and that would sooth my soul. One day three years later, my mother showed me an airline ticket. I couldn't believe my eyes. She had bought me a ticket to Texas to go be with my Dad.

I was elated. I was really going to see my Dad, the greatest man in the world to me. So, at age ten, I was flying to Texas. My mother had hired a chaperone to make sure that I would be safe on the flight. My chaperone checked on me from time to time but from what I could tell she wasn't worried about me much. Once we landed, my chaperone and I waited in the arrivals area for my father to pick me up. Though it had only been three years since I had last seen him, it seemed like a lifetime.

As soon as I stepped off the plane, I thought I saw him everywhere as I looked out at the brown, dry cityscape. Finally, when my Dad arrived at the terminal, I ran to him and hugged him as hard as I could. After the chaperone checked my Dad's identity she released me into his custody. Arriving at last at my Dad's one-bedroom apartment I finally felt relaxed: I was with my father, safe, and for the moment at peace. My Dad enrolled me in our neighborhood school. During my six-month stay with my Dad, I had the time of my life.

On the weekends, we would go crabbing and fishing. We never caught many fish but always caught plenty of crabs. After we netted our fill of crabs we would head home and cook them up for dinner. One memory I still cherish is that we always sat down and ate together. It's funny how these daily 30-minute dinners strengthened our father-son relationship. My father also taught me how to cook my first meal.

Every day after he came home from work he would call me into the house. I really hated this because he would stop me from doing my favorite thing, which at the time, was riding my bike. So every day for about two weeks I would watch my Dad cook. During our cooking lessons he would quiz me on spices and vegetables, and their uses for cooking and flavor. The first meal my Dad taught me how to cook was corned beef and rice. I don't know why that was the first meal he taught me how to cook—I'm guessing it wasn't too difficult a meal for a ten-year-old to prepare.

About a week after playing kitchen apprentice, it was time for me to prove myself. That evening I went into the kitchen alone, I first gathered up everything I needed to prepare my meal. One can corned beef, one small can of tomato paste, cooking oil, rice, salt, black pepper, red pepper, an onion, and a green bell pepper.

As I began cutting the onion, my eyes instantly began to water. The kitchen was small with dingy white walls and old brown cabinets that I hated opening due to the roaches which weren't like the ones in Boston. These Texas roaches were on steroids and would swipe your food if you didn't fight for it. I reached for the small stainless-steel pot with the burnt bottom and melted handle and filled it halfway with water. I stared at the water until it began to boil, then poured in my half cup of rice and turned the fire to low.

I turned on the frying pan and waited for the oil to heat. When I heard the oil pop I knew it was time to add the onions and green peppers. Turning the fire low, I remembered every step my father had taught me. Next it was time to add the tomato paste. Opening its can was my most difficult task because we didn't have a can opener.

I grabbed the biggest knife in the kitchen and positioned the tip in the groove at the edge of the can. I held the handle of the knife with my left hand as hard as I could struck it with the palm of my right hand. The pain in the palm of my hand caused me to belt out a curse. "Shit!" I yelled as I whacked the knife handle again. At last, the tip of the knife sank through the top of the can and I began sawing away at the metal. This process was slow and strenuous with the knife constantly slipping.

The can was finally opened, and I poured the tomato sauce into the pan with the onions and green peppers. A bead of sweat dropped from my nose and I turned off the rice which turned out pretty good. Soft, white, fluffy, I poked the fork in the pot and lifted out a few grains. I was so hungry I forgot to blow on the rice and burned my tongue. It stung for the next 30 seconds. The tomato paste, onions, and green pepper gave the kitchen and sweet aroma. It was now time to add the corned beef. Dinner was almost done.

I went through the steps exactly as I was taught. After 40 minutes of hard labor I was ready to serve up my first meal. As my Dad and I sat down and ate, not much was said. He mostly just ate and I mostly just watched him, trying to read some sort of expression about his thoughts on my meal. Finally, he put his fork down and looked over at me for a moment or two, then, a smile broke out across his mouth. He told me the food was good, and he was proud of me.

Finally I asked him why he had made me learn how to cook. He replied, "How can you eat if you can't cook? What if your girlfriend or wife doesn't know how to cook? What are you going to eat, McDonald's every day?" I just smiled back, comforted that my Dad was preparing me for life.

I was having the time of my life. I didn't care for the elementary school I was going to at the time, being that I was, like, the fifth Black kid in a school of White kids taught by White teachers who had not had the benefit of a racially-egalitarian education. For example, in music class the teacher mumbled "stupid Nigger" when I messed up. But the thought of riding one of the best bicycle models made that year—my Redline dirt bike—helped me through the tough days of being a new student in their "uneducated" education system.

My Dad bought the Redline for me when I first came to live with him, in Texas. A few weeks after moving to Texas I met a kid named Rex who also had a cool Mongoose dirt bike, with white pegs on the front and back wheels, which made it easier to do tricks while riding. Rex and I became close friends racing around on our bikes through the neighborhood I lived in with my dad. This was strange to me at the time, because he was White, and I was Black. Growing up in Boston, all my friends we're Black and living in my neighborhood where, if you weren't Black, you were Hispanic. As I think about it now, Rex was the first White friend I had, yet we became good friends instantly despite our different backgrounds. Rex would always visit me at my house, but for some reason Rex never invited me to his house, nor did I ever meet any of his family members. I never really thought about it at the time, and honestly it never crossed my mind to ask Rex how come we never hung out at his house. Probably because we were too busy having fun on our bikes bunny hopping and hitting wheelies.

One day after riding our bikes until the sun went down, my Dad decided we were going to give Rex a ride home because it was really dark, and he also lived quite a distance from my house. My Dad told Rex he could leave his bike at our house for the night, and we all piled into the car. On our way there everything seemed fine until the police pulled my Dad over and arrested him for driving while under the influence of alcohol. As my Dad was getting arrested, I was sitting in the back seat of our car with Rex who was looking at me like "what the fuck" and all I could do was stare blankly, disbelieving what I saw. It was one of my most painful, humiliating childhood memories.

After the officer cuffed and stuffed my Dad into the police car, then he returned to the car to ask us questions, who were we, where we were going? and some more bullshit questions that all sounded to me like blah blah blah. The whole time the police officer was talking to us I just stared through the glass at my Dad sitting in the center of the back seat of the squad car behind us. I was in shock or mortified, probably both. Another police car pulled up. After the two officers talked to each other for a while one of them walked back to my Dad's car and asked my friend Rex if I could go to his house. Rex's response was, "I guess so." As we were being put in the back seat of the second police car I looked at my Dad one last time with tears in my eyes. The ride through the night to Rex's house seemed like the longest ride of my life.

At about 10:30 p.m., we finally arrived at Rex's ranch style house with a big white front door. Once out of the police car, the cop didn't even wait for us to go inside before he pulled away. Rex and I stood at his front door for a while in complete silence. Finally, he turned to me with a terrified look on his face and said, "We have to be very quiet." He unlocked the door and we stepped inside.

The house was pitch black. He told me he would be right back and tiptoed away; I stood as still as a statue barely even breathing. When Rex returned to living room he had a fuzzy blanket and two pillows, and we lay down in silence and went to sleep on the carpet. I awoke that morning and didn't see Rex. Then from the end of the long hallway, I heard the sound of someone getting beaten accompanied by Rex's muffled cries, "I'm sorry!" followed by an adult's voice I will never forget, hissing angrily, "You brought a fucking nigger in my house." Quickly, I put on my shoes and slid out the sliding glass door behind the couch.

I walked until I found the main street and headed toward the house of a friend of my Dad. I arrived at my Dad's friend's house and used his phone to call my mom. My Dad didn't have a phone and this friend is where we would go once a week, so I could call her. When I told my Mom what happened she was hysterical; I told her

I would be okay, and my Dad would probably be home that day. She told me she was going to send for me as soon as she could and that everything would be okay. Ultimately, I was home alone for about ten days.

My Dad's friend told me as soon as he heard something about my Dad he would let me know, and I could come to his house every day to call my Mom. I walked back to my Dad's apartment, and just sat on the couch for a while. I started to get hungry as I watched my Dad's and my favorite show McGuyver. I thank God, my Dad taught me how to make corned beef and rice. During my ten days alone, I mostly just rode my bike and watched TV. I also used my Dad being in jail as an excuse not to go back to that racist elementary school I hated so much. Rex never came back to visit with me or to ask what happened or to retrieve his bike. It just stood there leaning against the far wall, a sad reminder of my situation. I never saw Rex again after the night my Dad was arrested. I worried about my Dad, and wondered what he was feeling while being in the county jail.

My ticket from my Mom finally arrived. My Dad was still in jail, so his friend brought me to the airport, and at age ten I flew alone back to Boston. For nearly two weeks, I had been on my own until the ticket arrived from my mother. I didn't see my Dad again until he returned to Boston two years later.

By 1991, the gang violence had escalated in Boston, and my mother was concerned for my safety, so she, decided to move to Oregon in an attempt to keep me from being killed, being that I had joined the "Shawmut Ave Boys" in 1989. A notorious street gang in the Roxbury section of Boston. In 1990 I shot myself in the hand playing with my cousin's gun and I also began selling drugs.

My mother had enough at that point and we left Boston. So over the next seven years I played a game of coastal ping pong between West Coast and East Coast. At age seventeen, I decided to remain in Boston with my Dad. I returned to Portland in 1995 on the run from Boston due to a shooting incident that happened during the summer in a heavily populated subway station in Roxbury.

After returning to Portland I met Neisy who would become the gentle-voiced mother of my children. In December of 1995 Neisy and I relocated back to Boston, and lived there for about 2 years. In

August of 1997 at age 21, pregnant girlfriend in tow, I returned to Portland. The week before I left, I bumped into a family friend who happened to be a Boston Police Detective. He asked me how my mother was, and I replied she was doing fine. Then next seven words that came out his mouth turned me white as a ghost, "you know there still looking for you." In one poetic motion I said, "nice seeing you," while spinning in the other direction walking away as fast as I could. At the time Neisy was six-months pregnant and then together a week later we returned to Portland.

In 1999, after a four-year relationship, Neisy and I broke up. There are many things I miss about her, not the least of which are her compassion, and her soft skin, and I take responsibility for the break-up. I was immature, spending my time running the streets and pursuing my addiction for money, alcohol, and drugs. Sad to say, my son was only two-years-old at the time.

Having already experienced life as the child of divorced parents, I had no intention for my son to experience any repercussions because of my decisions. My son and I were very close, not only after he was born, but I was very close to him while he was in the womb.

I was proud to be a father, and I cared for his mother while she was pregnant. I was there during labor and cut his umbilical cord at his birth. I remember the thrill of bringing Hakeem home and my family's excitement. He was the first grandchild in our family, and there was nothing but love surrounding his birth and my new fatherhood.

So without hesitation, I continued to raise my son after his mother and I separated. Really the only difference was that I no longer lived with his mother, but I was never far away. I kept my son every weekend, and anytime I had a day off from hustling. His mother and I really worked together to keep him protected from the negative effects of our break-up. In essence we practiced co-parenting. We never fought about who should raise our son, because we agreed that he needed both parents.

November 1, 2001, I began serving my 70-month sentence for second degree robbery. All of sudden reality hit me: Would I ever see my own father again? His health was deteriorating due to alcohol abuse. On November 18, 2005, eight days after Hakeem's 8th birthday, my father passed away from alcohol related illness. It was a painful day, especially since one of my plans had been to bring Hakeem to visit my father. Hakeem was his first grandchild. While I had been incarcerated, I wrote regularly to my father; I wanted to let him know my feelings and how much I appreciated him having been the best father he could have been to me. Not a day goes by that I don't miss him, but daily I thank him for never closing the door on our relationship.

My father passed in his sleep. My sister discovered his body when she came to visit him that morning which she did daily to make sure he was eating. She told me that he had my letters from prison spread around him. It gives me some small comfort that my Dad was rereading the letters that I had written to him before he died. This is a brief glimpse of the relationship between my father and me. It is one that I will always treasure and reflect upon. I share my childhood to give you an understanding of what I experienced as a child, and how this influenced the father that I chose to become, and the sacredness between my son and me.

The break-up with my girlfriend bought back memories of my own childhood all too clearly. It made me remember the relationship that my father and I had had. Though my Dad loved me, we didn't have the best relationship, and I wanted better for my son and me. It's hard to put a finger on it, but deep inside of me I knew I had to do the right thing, which was to be there for my son, no matter what.

By the time I was arrested for robbery in 2001, Hakeem's mother had remarried. I didn't care for her new husband and he didn't like me much either. I guess it was the fact that I was a good father, involved in my son's life, which meant he had to deal with me on some level. It seemed like her new husband had an attitude every time I called to speak with my son or his mother. I think he resented the fact that I remained involved in my son's life as best I could, despite my circumstances. Truthfully, I think her husband thought she still had feelings for me. Hakeem's mother had no choice but to interact with me, and even though we had had a rocky past, I still was consistently a good father to Hakeem and respectful to his mother.

So many nights, I sat in my cell wondering what my son was doing. Was he happy, was he being mistreated now that I wasn't there to spend time with him and protect him? Did he miss me? Would he still love me? So, I prayed to God, something I neglected to do when I was on the streets, much as I should have. I asked God to watch over my son, to protect him and help him to remember that I loved him and not to forget about me.

Chapter Two
Our First Visit

I COULDN'T BELIEVE THAT I was going to prison for five years and ten months. Five years and ten months away from my son: How would he manage without me? And how would I manage being away from him?

Hakeem was only three-and–a-half-years-old, so the concept of time was beyond his comprehension. Then I had his mother to consider and her thoughts on this whole situation. Would she become spiteful because I was locked up? Especially since now all financial burdens lay on Neisy concerning Hakeem's welfare. No doubt there are plenty of women out there who feel that if a father loved his child, he would not have gotten locked up in the first place. So why should she allow the child to make prison visits.

To make matters worse, we were arguing a lot—mostly because of her husband's jealousy. I thought, shit, she might even try to make my son call this man Daddy. Oh God, please don't let that happen; that thought alone was killing my spirit. I really didn't think I could make it through this ordeal, but I had no choice. Unless I could win in the appeals court and get my case overturned, this was it.

The ride from the courthouse back to the county jail was only about 20 minutes, but it felt like I'd been on the bus for hours. Once we were off the bus we were strip-searched and sent back to our units. I went straight to my bunk. For the last hour I hadn't said much to anyone. I'd just been lying on my bunk trying to shut my mind off. I was supposed to be getting a visit from my mother and my son that evening. I soon learned that once sentenced, there was no telling when I would leave for Intake, which is the way station before you go to the penitentiary (a/k/a) The Big House.

Dinner time came around and I just lay on my bunk. When I grew tired of staring at the cold gray cement walls, I began to concentrate on the low hum from the dim light mounted above my head. The depression was sinking in. After dinner, my name was called for a visit. I combed my hair and waited in the sallyport for my escort who arrived and patted me down. I forgot I had an aspirin in my shirt pocket, so they sent me back to the sallyport to determine my fate.

The sallyport is an 8x10 cement box with white walls and two sliding metal doors on either side, each with a 4x4 window. This area is the gateway between inmate housing units and the rest of county jail. This area is usually littered with paper, pencils, trash, and other forms contraband. When leaving the unit, an inmate is not to take anything with him. Once he enters the sallyport anything in his possession is considered contraband.

As I waited for the unit officer to let me back in the unit, another deputy walked by and asked me what I was waiting for. I told him I had a visitor, so he brought me down to the visiting room. But before I could walk in with the rest of the inmates, the visiting officer called my name. I stepped out of the line and asked him what was up. He told me my visit had been cancelled because I had contraband in my pocket. Then he told me I could go to the hole for this infraction. At this point all the stress and anger I had been holding in for the last two months finally boiled over. I told the officer, "I don't give a fuck what you do. I'm on my way to the pen anyway!"

So off to the hole I went. Powerless, I just didn't care anymore, which had always been one of my biggest problems. Once I lost my temper I didn't think about the consequences. The next morning they woke me up in Solitary Confinement and told me I was leaving for the Intake Center. The Intake Center is where all sentenced inmates with state time go for evaluations. The counselors there assess inmates' mental health, physical health, and educational level, and then decide which prison to send them to. Prisoners can spend anywhere from seven to thirty days, and sometimes even longer, in the Intake Center.

This was a really stressful time because, while I was in Intake, I couldn't receive visits or buy anything from the commissary: No toothpaste, lotion, or any other hygiene products. All I could do was use the phone and stress about what prison they'd be shipping me off to. Worst case scenario, I would go to Snake River Correctional Institution which was seven hours away from Portland where my son and family lived. The best-case scenario was that I'd get sent to Oregon State Penitentiary which was only forty-minutes away from Portland.

Luckily, I only had to spend seven days in the Intake Center. The day I was leaving to be shipped to my institution, all my hopes were stepped on and kicked to the curb. All inmates who were leaving got lined up and guards began shackling us with wrist, ankle, and body chains. Then they started calling out last names and institutions. The three people ahead of me were going to Oregon State Penitentiary. I said to myself, God, please let me go to Oregon State Penitentiary.

Then they called my name, "Bossman," and I responded, "Right here." And that's when the hammer fell: They said I was going to Two Rivers Correctional Institution. Damn, I thought I might never see my son! Two Rivers was located three hours away from Portland and it was a newly-built facility, barely open one year. Plus Two Rivers is in Umatilla, which is made up of red necks and crackers who have limited experience working with African-Americans. The majority of the officers were from that area, so I was reasonably confident they would be racist! I'd heard some stories about Black inmates being mistreated by racist guards at the Two Rivers facility, and again I was reasonably confident it wouldn't be long before I was back in the hole.

About two weeks had passed since I had seen my son. I wondered how he was doing. I missed him to death, his high energy, his silliness, his thoughtful gestures, everything. But right then I had to prepare myself mentally for what lay ahead of me. From what I knew about prisons, the conditions are never good and I worried about what to expect since this was my first time in prison. All I could think was the first motherfucker to try me is getting knocked out. I had known a lot of people who did time, and from what I recalled they all said the same thing, "Don't take shit from anybody."

When we finally arrived at Two Rivers Correctional Facility, I had resigned myself to the fact that this was now my new home for the next five years and ten months. Surrounded by razor wire, the sight of the prison itself was depressing, and the desert stretched as far as the eye could see. The transport officers marched us all in and we were dressed down into prison blues and then sent to the Administrative Orientation Unit, or A & O.

The Two Rivers institution was and probably still is the worst one in the state because it is a closed custody facility. Closed custody means that inmates only get to interact with the people in their unit. With a total of 15 units in this institution, one of them was the AD Segregation Unit—a/k/a solitary confinement. Each unit housed 104 inmates, and is self-contained with a recreational yard, and dayroom, which also contains a chow hall, a barber station, two classrooms and eight showers. The only time inmates are allowed to leave the unit is for medical purposes, visits, education in the education department, religious services in the chapel, or a job that's not on the unit such as, a kitchen worker, maintenance worker, laundry sorter or canteen worker. Other than that, inmates stayed confined to their unit.

As soon as I got to the A & O Unit, the portly Sergeant with an overgrown mustache pointed me in the direction of my assigned cell. Once there, I made my bed and put away what little property I had, mainly state issued clothing and court documents from my trial, but no personal effects, no photo of my son. My cellmate was an older Black brother in his fifties with a secretive look in his eyes. We exchanged greetings and names, but after that not much else was said.

I hadn't talked with my family in over a week, so after making my bed and getting my things in order I left my cell and headed straight for the payphone. I dialed my mother's phone number, and after a few rings she picked up. When the phone recording finished giving instructions, my mother pressed the number five button to accept my collect call. I told her where I'd been moved to and what it was like so far. I asked how my brother and sisters were doing and she told me everyone was fine.

It's funny how small things like that put Kool-Aid smiles on my face. I then asked her if she had seen my son, and she told me

Hakeem had been over a few days before. I asked her if he still remembered me and she assured me that he did. I told her I needed everyone's information, so I could put in the visiting forms. Then I told her about the special consent form Hakeem's mother needed to fill out and get notarized before my son could come and see me.

We continued to talk for a while. I asked her to send me some photos of my son and of the family. Then the automated phone voice stated we had one-minute left. We said our goodbyes and I asked her to give the rest of my family my love. Then the phone went dead. My next move was to the file box that held all the different forms for inmates. Such as grievance forms, medical forms, and forms for religious service just to name a few.

I searched out the visitor's applications and collected the required amount need for all my visitors. I got back to my cell, sat down at the desk, and began to fill them out. As I was completing the visitor's forms, I thought about the photos of my son and my family that my mother was going to send. A mental picture of Hakeem appeared in my head, how he was always cheerful, and wiggly, how his hair smelled of Dax Green Hair Wax, and I began to smile. Just the thought of being able to look at pictures of my son helped me forget about my depressing environment.

Two and a half weeks without seeing Hakeem's face, or hearing his warm voice seemed like a lifetime and I'm a grown man; I couldn't even imagine what it felt like for him. To make matters worse I couldn't even call to see how he was doing, because his mother's phone didn't accept collect calls. Even though his mother and I weren't on the best terms, she still had a certain amount respect for me.

I believe this because no matter what, I always took care of my son. I thought I should probably write her a letter just to tell her that I was sorry for leaving her with the burden of raising our son alone. And to let her know all that I ask of her is to let my mother bring my son to come see me. Deep down she knew I was a good person and I believed she would do the right thing, and not be spiteful and keep my son away from me. If she did, that would really hurt, but it would hurt my son even more. As his parents, we needed to do what was best for our child no matter how we felt or what resentment we might have harbored toward each other due to actions in the past. I have since learned that is called sublimating your ego in order to do whatever is in your child's best interest.

Some people believe prison is no place for a child to be exposed to especially when one of the parents is an inmate. Most feel this way due to the fear of the mental scarring it could leave on a child. Yet I have come to believe it's more damaging to a child's psyche when she/he is denied a relationship with a parent. No matter what the circumstance, as long as the child's safety isn't in danger, giving a child the opportunity to be loved by his/her parent or parents can make a world of difference in the child's life.

Two more weeks passed, and I still hadn't gotten a response on the status of the visitation forms I had submitted. The counselor informed me that it could take up to 30 days to be processed and approved. They say patience is a virtue, but all I could think was, they just need to hurry the hell up. The day before, I received some pictures of my son, plus some of my mom, brothers, and sisters. I feel bad admitting this, but I looked at the pictures of my family for a hot second, and went straight to the pictures of my son. It was heart wrenching, and my sadness immediately turned to anger because I realized I was completely powerless, and truthfully, I almost broke down in tears. For about five minutes I just stared at Hakeem's pictures and analyzed every aspect of him, like the way his eyes would squint up just like mine whenever he smiled. I began remembering our times together and how he made me feel, like I was on top of the world. How he depended on me to show him how to ride his bike, and the joy I felt watching him be happy. Just by looking at the clothes he was wearing in the picture, I could go back in my mind and remember what we did together the day he wore the outfit.

I decided to call my mother and thank her for the pictures. After a few minutes talking about this and that, she told me to hold on. The next five letters I heard over the phone brought tears to my eyes: "Daddy?!" It was Hakeem's voice calling out my name. For a second I choked on my words as they came out, "How's my big boy?" He asked me where I was, and when he was going to see me again.

I skipped the first of his questions and answered the second. I told him that we would be seeing each other very soon. The day after my son had turned four-years-old, I'd arrived at Two Rivers Correction Facility. I asked him about his birthday party and all the present's he got. Then I asked him what kind of present he wanted me to get him.

He, being the same great kid I left, said he wanted some wrestling action figures. This statement brought back more memories of us playing together and how I would let him beat me up. Before I ended our conversation, I told him no matter what, I would always love him and I would always be his Dad. Then I told him to remember to be a good boy and to listen to his Mom and his Grandma. He told me he loved me too, and that he missed me. Then my mother got back on the phone. I told her as soon as they were approved for visiting, I would call.

That night as I lay in my bed, I replayed those beautiful words my son said to me, "I love you and miss you." They played over and over in my head, like a CD on repeat. A few days later my son and my family members were approved to come visit me. I called my mother on a Tuesday and she said they would be out there that coming Sunday. I gave her the visiting hours and the dress code for visitors, and how many visitors I could have at one time. I barely got any sleep the rest of the week. All I could think about was seeing my family. All together it totaled about a month since I had last seen my son.

That Sunday morning I woke up at 6:30 a.m., and got ready for my visit that was at 7:00 a.m. After I got dressed I sat down and watched the clock in the day room. When 7:30 am came, I began to panic, even though I knew my mother was late for everything I was still thinking the worst. I love my mother, but truth be told, she'll be late for her own funeral.

Then they called my name over the P.A. system, "Bossman, you have a visit.

Chapter 2: PARENTING POINTS

+ Find ways to adjust, like prayer, meditation, exercise, or other peaceful actions that bring you to a calm state in your new environment.

+ Channel negative energy by focusing on ways to best accommodate your child.

+ Ask if your facility has any special service for inmates' children and family.

+ Make a joy list of things that give you a sense of peace, like your child's smile—things for which you're thankful.

Chapter Three

The Visiting
Room

I WALKED INTO THE VISITING room and asked myself how

they expect small children to play in these cramped conditions.

There were about 15 smallish chairs in each row, with a total of six

rows. Now these weren't the comfortable chairs that you might sit

in at a five-star restaurant. No, no, no, these were hard plastic

chairs, with square metal legs. The chairs were in groups of two,

three, or four and in between each group of chairs were these small white square boxes. The boxes were about eight inches wide and eight inches high.

The guard walking me into the visiting room told me that I had to stay seated at all times, except when my family came in. He said I could hug and kiss my family at the beginning of the visit and at the end of the visit. My child was the only one I could have constant contact with during the visit. Then he pointed out the group of chairs my family was to sit in, and the chair directly across was where I was to sit. I took my seat and waited for my family.

After about five minutes of waiting, a side door in the visiting room opened and families began to pour in. I shifted in my seat a little to get a better view of the door that the visitors were coming in. Mom's Elizabeth Taylor White Diamonds perfume told me she was there before I saw her. Then the comforting sound of my mother's gold African-style earrings tinkling reminded me of her, back home, cleaning the house while listening to music; her earrings somehow always made a song of their own as she moved with the beat. And now she was moving along ushering in my son and siblings, still obscured from my sight by other visitors.

Entering the visiting room, my mother stood there regally in her colorful African head wrap and called out my name. Her voice reached out and grabbed me and pulled me right out of that dark place.

With her were my four-year-old sister and my nine-year-old brother, and at last I saw the face I had waited so long to see. I stood up and waved at everyone. My son and I locked eyes and he let go of my mother's hand and ran to me and jumped straight at me, like a rocket launcher. I grabbed him out of the air and hugged him tightly and kissed him all over his face. His clothes smelled of Bounce Dryer Sheets as he buried his face under my chin and hugged me. All I could say was, "my little boy, my little baby boy I missed you so much."

The rest of my family approached us, and we all hugged for a few seconds. When I kissed my mom on her cheek it was still as silky smooth as when I was a kid. We all sat down, and Hakeem looked at me with his same beautiful smile and I kissed him on the forehead. Seeing the joy on both our faces, my mother shed a tear. Then, we talked about the three-hour ride to the prison, and some of the nice scenery along the way. She told me how the last hour of the ride was all desert, and how depressing and cold the prison looked from the outside.

My little brother took my son and my baby sister to get some toys from the sparsely populated shelf known as the toy section. My mother told me how good it was to see me. I told her how much I missed her and the family. She asked me if I wanted anything from the snack or soda machine. I think she was nervous and wanted to switch the subject. I told her a juice would be fine, and that she should get something for the children to eat and drink.

Just for the record, my mother is a health nut, so she immediately complained when she saw that the snack machine was filled with nothing but junk food and the beverage machine contained soda and the kind of juice made mostly of corn syrup. So she bought the most healthful items she could find, which were a couple lemonades and a few bags of chips. The kids were delighted to see the snacks and immediately began devouring them. I really didn't want my son to sit on the floor, but he basically insisted by squirming around in my lap until he could slither off. So I let him down to the floor to play with the two cars he had from the toy section. Automatically Hakeem passed me one of the cars so I could play with him. I bent over in my chair and played his game of crash the cars.

As time went by, I realized I'd been neglecting the rest of my family, so I began rotating conversations between my little brother, sister, and mother. This was no easy task, because my son kept calling Daddy, Daddy, Daddy when I started losing in the game we were playing. Add the fact that my son and my little sister are two months apart in age. My sister is the older of the two, and they were beginning to overwhelm me by competing with each other to see who could get the most attention from me. I don't know how this feud started between them, but it became serious. I asked my brother to go get a board game, so everyone could feel involved and receive equal attention. He came back with CandyLand and we all began to play. This was a great idea, because it kept my son and sister occupied which allowed me to have a conversation with my mother.

I began telling her about prison, and how racist the guards

were. I described my day-to-day routine, from working out, to eating meals and adjusting to sharing a small cell with a stranger. I could tell she was getting sad by the detailed description of prison life, so I changed the subject. I asked her how her organization was doing, and how my family in Boston was doing.

The visit was going a little too fast for me. I checked the clock and only 45 minutes remained before the visit was to end. My son climbed back up onto my lap to play CandyLand, and I asked him how he liked his school. He said that he liked it a lot and told me about all the things he was learning, about all his friends, and the pictures he had drawn for me. I asked him how high he could count, and he began counting. He made it to 30 and then I joined in, and we both continued until we reached 50. Since the visit was almost over, I wanted to make our time together as memorable as possible until our next visit.

My brother put the board game away, and my son and I played together with some action figures. A few minutes later the guard announced that visits were ending in the next five minutes. My mother told my little brother and sister to throw away the trash, and put the rest of the toys away. I told my son how much I missed him and that I loved him. Then I tickled him and kissed him on the head. I felt it would be hard on him when it was time to leave, so I was trying to keep him in a positive state of mind. Then I heard those dreaded words, "Visiting is now over."

I stood up with my son in my arms, and hugged my brother and sister. I told them that I missed them already and to be good. Then I gave my mother a hug and kissed her on the cheek and thanked her for bringing my son and family to see me. She told me she'd be back in a month. I looked to my son and noticed the change his face displayed. His expression was now one of confusion. I said to him that it was time to leave. When my words registered he laid his head on my shoulder. I told him I would see him soon and that I loved him, and to be a good boy. When he lifted his head from my shoulder tears were falling from his eyes. I tried my hardest to hold back my tears, but one escaped. I wiped it away quickly and smiled. My son told me he didn't want to leave. I told him he would be back and we'd see each other soon and everything would be okay. My mother helped me out and took my son from my arms and told him they'd be back soon. Then my family started toward the exit with the rest of the families. I waved at them and they waved back until they were out of sight.

As I watched them leave the visiting room I felt a mixture of happiness and sadness. The feeling of sadness came from the pain I saw in Hakeem's eyes when it was time to leave; nonetheless, I was happy that I was able to see him and my family. I thought I could handle this bid, but suddenly I was not so sure.

At that point I came to realize that only through God's grace and strength would I make it. It wouldn't be an easy road to travel but I knew that I had to stay strong for Hakeem's sake.

As soon as all the visitors had left the visiting room, the guard told all the inmates to line up against the wall. He began calling out names and inmates stepped up to grab their identification cards. When he got to my name I stepped up to take my I.D. card. He handed it to me but told me to stand back up against the wall. After all the other inmates left, four other inmates and I were taken to a bathroom and strip-searched thoroughly one by one.

By now I was used to being dehumanized and humiliated. I

went through the motions as directed by the officer. Once the search was completed I got dressed and headed back to my unit, reminiscing about my son and family and how good it was to see them. I entered my unit, headed straight to my cell, and took off my visiting clothes. I hung up my light blue button-down shirt and put my navy blue denim jeans back under my mattress—this kept them straight and creased.

Redressed back into my daily slightly worn-looking clothes, I lay on my bunk thinking about how much time I had left on my bid. Damn, I was only at the beginning. How was I going to be a father to my son for the next 67 months? Due to the distance of the prison, I would probably see him only once a month. I could write him letters, but he was not old enough to read yet. Then there was the chance that his mother wouldn't read the letters to him, or that her husband might get jealous seeing my name addressed to his wife and throw it away.

I couldn't call him, because Neisy's phone didn't accept collect calls. And even if I got through, our situation being what it is, would probably lead to an argument before I would even get to talk to my son. With all the obstacles and hurdles that kept popping up, I was like, "fuck it" and closed my eyes to go to sleep before I got a headache.

I took a deep breath and told myself that I couldn't give up. I have to persevere for Hakeem's sake. He needed me more than ever and, as it was, I had already let him down by going to prison. I knew I had to find a way to still be there for him and provide the love and protection he needed from me—his father.

With my eyes closed I took deep, slow breaths through my nose and blew out slowly through my mouth. After about three minutes of this I felt a little better. Later on that night I would call my mother and see if they made it back safely. Plus, I wanted to find out how my son had acted when they left. Did he cry more on the way back, and what did he say about seeing me? He might even be at her house and I could talk to him and tell him what a great time I had seeing him and playing together. As I thought back on my visit I felt bad because I had neglected to really give my brother and sister my full attention. Just a few hours left before I can call, I thought. I knew I had to stop looking at the clock or I'd drive myself crazy.

Chapter 3: PARENTING POINTS

- ✦ Give your child or children time to warm up to you being in a prison. The first time is difficult for anyone.

- ✦ Be sure to plan ahead, and find activities that involve all your visitors.

- ✦ Talk about and do things with your child or children that will make your visit as—happily—memorable as possible.

- ✦ Ask questions. Listen twice as much as you talk—God gave us two ears and one mouth for a reason!

- ✦ Hug and kiss your child or children at the end of your visit. Remind them you are okay and that no matter what you love them.

- ✦ Use the positive feeling you got from seeing your child or children to help you stay focused until your next visit with them.

=

Chapter Four
A Fathers Duty

WHAT IS A FATHERS DUTY? What is his responsibility to his child? How does he learn what the essentials are to this title if his own father wasn't around to be his example?

For me fatherhood is a day-to-day learning experience. I believe as the world changes so do some of the rules. But there are some rules that never change, like unconditional love, sacrifice, and understanding. These are just some of the basic rules, but it takes more than these few actions to raise a child properly. A father's role extends to future generations. Everything he passes down to his child will carry on for decades.

It is imperative that a father must remain a positive role model for his child. From birth he's observed closely by his child. A male will want to be like his father and a female will want her husband to be like her father if he is a positive role model. For instance, in one study, preschool-age children whose fathers were responsible for 40% or more of the family's child care tasks had higher scores on assessments of cognitive development, had more of a sense of mastery over their environments, and exhibited more empathy than those children whose fathers were less involved (Volume 2 Number 1, Spring 2001 University of California, Division of Agriculture & Natural Resources, Author Margaret Johns). Proper guidance and molding must begin from the start.

I used to have the notion that if I bought my child everything he wanted all the time, he would love and respect me more. But you can't buy your child's love, respect, or admiration. The bribery method will only teach your child to over value material things.

The first stage of a father's duty is to create a positive and healthy environment for the child to grow in. This means a drug-free home and a home that holds spirituality and is run by good morals and values, with both parents respecting each other.

The second stage is teaching the child what it takes to be a leader, and that s/he should never let others (such as peers) make decisions for them. Instilling the importance of a good work ethic and the value of education, and teaching children the history of their ancestors and their struggles will help give your child a sense of achievement and pride.

The third stage is spirituality, and helping your children understand that there is a power greater than themselves, and that accountability is essential—I believe it is essential for a child to understand that our actions will not only be judged in this life, but when we leave this earth. It's important for your child to feel that s/he has a purpose in this life, and when that child has fulfilled a unique and personal purpose then s/he has achieved true success, because spirituality maintains balance, inner peace, and mental growth.

The fourth stage of a father's duty is exposing his child to the benefits of financial independence. How having a bank account is important, and saving money and understanding the differences between a checking and saving account. A parent should instill the importance of keeping good credit and judicious use of credit cards. And be clear why it's important to pay bills and debts on time and not let them become overdue. Then there's the owning of property, which I think is most important, when educating your child on personal finances. This knowledge is beneficial because property can be passed on to future generations. After food, shelter is the second most important factor to support a human's existence. Shelter can protect you from the elements of nature, from danger, and can be used as a storage facility, and even a business.

Then there is employment, which includes teaching your child how to apply for a job, what to wear, and what to say. Educating children on self-employment is also important as it gives individuals the power to determine their own financial destiny. Children should understand that if they work for someone else, they will always be limited in how far they are able to advance in the ranks of any company. By owning one's own company, family members can be employed, and when a family works together the possibilities for success become endless.

The fifth stage is personal health, and education on the diseases that affect your race at a higher rate than other races. For African Americans, for example, high cholesterol, high blood pressure, and diabetes are some of the more common health issues. So teaching your child how to eat healthy and maintain a balanced diet is important. Also important is physical exercise and staying fit which helps fight diseases and keeps the immune system strong.

Sex is probably the hardest subject for parents to talk to their children about, but it is important to educate them about safe sex. Let's be honest: It would be nice if our children would remain abstinent until marriage, but that may not be a realistic expectation. So we must teach them the proper way to use contraceptives in order for them to be effective in the protection of sexually transmitted diseases and unwanted pregnancies. I still believe the best safe sex contraceptive is no sex. I hate to sound so old fashioned, but, as an African American myself, I have learned that for African Americans this is a serious issue, as we have the highest rate of teen pregnancy and HIV infections. I guarantee that no parent wants to see their child die a slow, painful death.

With these five basic stages taught and ingrained in a child's mind you are on your way to fulfill your duty as a father. But never forget your example is the best teacher of all. Be conscious of your actions even when you think your child or children aren't watching or listening. Also don't be afraid to admit to your child when you are wrong about something. Another important element that a lot of parents don't think is a big deal—but it is—is being a friend to your child. To me this is the major part of communication between parent and child. If your children always see you as a constant authoritarian, they will be more apt to hide things from you. An open line of communication goes a long way.

Sometimes it's hard seeing our children grow up and doing grown up things that we as parents don't agree with. This can sometimes make it hard for us to listen to their issues without criticizing them. But remember that listening is the quickest path to understanding. Spending time with your child is also important especially if you have more than one child, because this gives each child personal time with parent or parents and no one feels left out.

Make time for family events or have a special day set out every week to do something together. And let your children pick the event sometimes. It's called family day because it takes the involvement of the whole family. In a day and age wherein parents are working longer shifts and more days, children are spending excessive amounts of time watching television or playing video games, on-line or doing things they shouldn't be doing. Family time is necessary because it instills family unity and promotes bonding.

It is also a father's duty to make sure he never puts himself in the position of being taken away from his child. For those who are granted the opportunity, once released from prison, it is every father's duty to do everything ethical within his power to remain free. Every parent has to take a hard look at what they are doing or planning to do and weigh whether it is more important than being there for their child. Would your child rather have the newest sneakers or have Dad and Mom free? Is being high for a few minutes or hours better than spending time with your child or helping them with their homework? Is staying out all night partying more important than staying home to tuck your child into bed to provide

a consistent sense of security?

My near-six-year experience in prison taught me a different set of priorities than I had before incarceration. There is nothing more important than the happiness of my child, but I can't contribute to that if I'm not there. Missing birthdays, first days of school, graduations, sporting events, award ceremonies, and just plain old good mornings and good nights are all crucial.

So, freedom is my first duty to my child, because not being there for him, is not fair to my son, and I am actually putting him in danger. That danger stems from not being able to teach him what he needs to know to survive and be successful in this world, and simply from not being there to protect him. My duty as a father is to never let my child see the "streets" as an option. To never have to look to his friends for guidance because I wasn't there to guide and advise him and show him how to avoid the traps and the bait of the street life which influence many, and lead most to make unwise decisions.

Since my incarceration, I have seen three generations of males from one family imprisoned all at the same time. Grandfather, son, and grandson, each father having failed his duty to his son, which led to his son and grandson making the same mistakes and carrying forward negative and debilitating traditions. This is why it's imperative to remain free. And, if your parents weren't there for you, I'm sorry, but now you're the adult in your equation. And as the adult, you're accountable. You can't blame your parents or your child or the system. Choose to be there. Be present. You're the boss.

Seeing two generations of men who were lost, because one man neglected his duty also served as a catalyst, providing inspiration for this book. Being a parent is not an easy job, and being a father is even harder, especially if you're African American, due to the racism that still plagues our country. It has become common for fathers to not be involved in the raising of their children. But no matter what society has deemed acceptable, you are responsible for ensuring your child has a future. You are the guardian of their well-being until they reach adulthood and become responsible for themselves.

Even then you still have a moral responsibility to them, because you will always be their parent, and they will always be your child.

A father is the head of the body, and the body is the family. So, the father must not only think of himself, but also how his actions will affect his family. My generation, known as Generation X, has to break the cycle of fathers being absent from the home. A lot of my peers, and I too, grew up with a father who was seldom around; this led to us idolizing the wrong people as role models. Most of the people we looked up to were pimps, drug dealers, and gangsters.

Unfortunately, when you grow up without a consistent father figure you look up to the most confident and respected men in your environment, irrespective of their ethics. It is important that the fathers from my generation don't pass on what we thought was correct information regarding what a man's responsibilities and duties are to his children and family. Most of us men—not just in my circle but men of every socio-ethno and socio-economic group— are taught to be unfaithful to women, never show your emotions, and do whatever it takes to get money, even if it means jeopardizing your freedom and life. Every one of these behaviors will lead to self-destruction, not only of self but also of your children and loved ones who are affected by your actions.

Everything in life can be easier, even the hard shit, if you break it down into smaller parts and deal with those one by one. Even being a parent. You can do everything; you just cannot do every single thing at the very same time. Mistakes will be made along the way, but as long as you put your children first, you can't go wrong. You will be doing your duty as a father, and you will also impact generations to come.

Countless children are jeopardized by one selfish parent who chooses to lob off his responsibilities to the system—the already-overburdened system that then must raise the child. Untold numbers of children's lives have wasted away due to improper guidance. I don't have all the answers, but I know for certain that simply by just being in your child's life you can make a difference. Your example as a positive figure and role model will give your child the skills needed to survive in this world.

Being a man doesn't mean making a baby. Being a man means providing for and raising that child to be all she/he can be.

Chapter 4: PARENTING POINTS

- Daily, throughout the day, make decisions that ensure you
- never jeopardize your freedom.
- Maintain a safe environment for your child/children.
- Support and provide for your child/children no matter your circumstances. Look for opportunities to trade on your skills.
- Be a positive example to your children, family, and for anyone who happens to be in your space.
- Most of all, love your child/children unconditionally.

Chapter Five

Financial Support

ONE OF THE HARDEST QUESTIONS I asked myself was how I could financially support my child from prison?

I didn't have a bank account with any money saved. The job the prison had issued me only paid $55 a month which was a barber for my unit, which there were a total of 2 . My only other source of income was from family members, who sent me money from time to time (monthly) when their budgets permitted. Luckily, I had one other source, a good friend of mine to whom I owe many thanks, my boy Kase. Some guys are fortunate enough when they do their time to have a wife or girlfriend, to provide them with some financial support but for me that wasn't the case.

A lot of men who are locked up and have children have this idea that because they are incarcerated and don't have a real job to pay them a substantial income, that they don't have a financial responsibility to their children. This is a selfish way of thinking. It's bad enough that prisoners did whatever they did to get put in prison, but to use it as an excuse to not give whatever monies you can to your child or children is plain ridiculous and unacceptable. Any financial help to your child's mother to help with the care of your child is a plus. This can also encourage her to help make it easier for you to have more interaction with your child during your incarceration. I can say from experience that this is true, because it lets the mother of your children know that you still want to be a part of their lives, and that you are not ducking your responsibility as a parent.

For the first year of my incarceration I didn't have any contact verbally by phone or through written correspondence with Hakeem's mother, but I did have her address so I was able to have money and anything else my son wanted or needed brought to his mother's house. I think by me still contributing financially without any communication to or with Hakeem's mother, showed her that I was still going to do my part the best way I could. Most importantly my son was able to see that I was still there for him. For me to be able to do small things for him, like buying presents for birthdays and other occasions, gave my son reassurance that I could be counted on. A promise to a child from a parent is very important to keep because it builds trust. Trust between a child and a parent is essential for good parenting to be effective. The stronger the trust, the easier it is for your child to accept advice from you.

Being that I was no millionaire I first had to figure out what my finances were on a monthly basis. I'd grab a sheet of paper and a pen and write down my monthly income and its sources. I received $55 dollars a month from my prison job and about $50 dollars from family members. This gave me a total of $105 dollars a month. For my basic survival I only needed about $50 dollars monthly for my hygiene products, envelopes, postage stamps, and food items from the commissary.

So, I decided that every other month I would try to send Hakeem's mother $50 dollars. To most people in the free world $50 dollars every other month isn't much, especially when it's being received as child support. But when you're a single parent every dollar counts. It's also a good thing to save your receipts for the duration of your sentence, plus seven years thereafter, just in case you need them for court purposes to prove you were paying child support, also of course in the unlikely event of a tax audit.

I knew birthdays and providing money for the new school year were a must. Summertime wardrobes were also important because by the time summer arrived, the clothing worn during the school year was either torn up or outgrown. One thing about young children and clothes, they never worry about being careful and keeping their clothes nice while playing.

I set challenges for myself, like, every three months I would ask my son what kind of toy he wanted, and then try to get it for him. My goal wasn't to spoil him or teach him that relationships were based on material items. My intention was only to make my presence felt as much as I could during my incarceration. I felt the more things my son had around him to remember me by the better. Nothing can take the place of a parent not being there, but you can do things to make sure you're not totally forgotten.

Of course, I knew that I was not forgotten but I also knew that it was my job to make sure my son was happy and still felt a sense of normalcy. I knew if I were there with him daily then he'd be happier than he already was. But since I wasn't, I wanted to do whatever I could to make him happy and reassure him that I would always be there. Some people believe this method is a form of spoiling your child. I see it as letting your child know that you love them, and will try to do what you can for them to the best of your ability no matter the circumstances or situation.

On one occasion, about two and half years into my sentence, I decided it was time to buy Hakeem another bike. He was five-years-old by this time, and the first bike I bought him was before I went to prison, he had now outgrown. The first bike was bought when my son was about three and had training wheels on it. So, I made a call to my friend who was like a brother to me, and holding me down financially through my bid, and told him my son needed a new bike. With his usual response, "Don't worry about it, it's taken care of" my son had his new bike on the way.

Once I had confirmation that Hakeem's bike had been delivered, I called his mother's house, and she put my son on the phone. I asked him if he got his new bike, and he replied "yes" in a joyful voice, and told me how all his friends wanted to ride it. I told him I was glad he liked it and to take care of it. To someone free, buying your child a bike probably isn't a big deal, but to me it was something major because I knew every time my son rode his bike he would think of me. I also made it a rule of thumb that anytime a hundred dollars or more was sent to my account, I would send half to Hakeem's mother. I made it a point to let her know that she could use it for whatever was needed. Even though I would have liked for her to buy my son some new clothes, shoes, or toys, I had to remember there were other things my child needed, like food in the refrigerator, a roof over his head, lights to see, and all the other things children take for granted. By telling Hakeem's mother she could use the money at her own discretion, I relieved any unnecessary pressure I may have put on her if I had asked her to buy specific things for my son. Plus, this form of parental respect is in the child's best interest; it's good role-modeling.

Most prisons have different programs available during the holiday season that you can sign your children up for. During Christmas time there was a program that allowed inmates to pick from a list of items which were then delivered to the home of your child. I advise anyone who is given the opportunity to partake in one of these programs, especially if you aren't able to provide things like toys, clothes, and other necessities for your child throughout the year. This could give you at least one outlet to do something for your child, giving them a positive memory to hold on to. The most important thing you can do for your child during your prison experience is keeping your connection and bond as strong as possible. A little sacrifice goes a long way, and truthfully what's more important than seeing your child happy?

A lot of inmates create side hustles to help them financially support their children. Some of these side hustles include doing art work and selling it, or helping other inmates with legal work. Some guys who have had a lot of time in prison and work out regularly offer personal weight training to other inmates. So, if you have any talents that can help you acquire extra finances it's a good idea to put them to use.

Another tactic that I have used is to save as much money as I can, and designate it to important calendar events, such as birthdays and the week before school starts—an important date for fathers who have children in school. One thing that I can say from experience is do not get too stressed out when you are not able to provide for your family and children financially, and then go and make a bad decision that leads you to do something that could get you more time. For those who have release dates, the most important thing is going home on time. And for those who do not, every visit you can have with your child, family and friends are a blessing, so do your best not to lose them by going to the hole. Being an incarcerated father providing financially for your child may be your hardest task, but all you can do is try your best to contribute, and contribute what you can, when you can. Set small goals for yourself; they add up.

Chapter 5: PARENTING POINTS

- Create a budget with any finances you receive. If possible, dedicate a portion for child support.
- You are still responsible for your child/children financially, so keep planning, keep trying.
- Contribute what you can, when you can.
- Sacrifice indulgence and save for your children's education and other important events.

Chapter Six

Communication

FOR EVERY INCARCERATED FATHER trying to keep a healthy relationship with his children, communication is essential. To be able to say I love you to your children and communicate that you are still there for them is food for emotional growth.

Communication comes in many forms. The most common form is spoken, then visual, touch, body language, and finally, written. Without communication, how can you express what you are feeling? Since phone calls from prison are very expensive, I suggest for any father who has a child able to read, letters are a good way of communicating. In my experience, communicating through letters is a good way for parents and children to express their feelings without feeling embarrassed. A lot of times, when face-to-face, or when you're talking with someone on the other end of the phone, your mind goes blank. I think that happens partially because you are so happy to see or hear from them that you forget what you planned to say. I know for myself, there were many times when I was so excited to see my son and family that I forgot everything that I planned to talk about.

Even families without a parent incarcerated have poor communication between parents and children, possibly because communication generally is not on any school's curriculum. So for fathers incarcerated, this puts us at an even greater disadvantage when it comes to keeping up a healthy dialogue with our children. A lot of us grew up not communicating in a healthy manner with our parents about our feelings and emotion. I thank God I had a nosey, caring mother who constantly asked me questions about how I was feeling emotionally. Because she cared, and was confidential, to this day I feel like I can talk to her about anything.

Growing up, young boys are taught early to hide our feelings. We are told things like, boys don't cry, or never show your feelings because feelings can you get killed, is something that was often said among men and boys in my culture growing up. Or that only sissy boys get emotional, or you have to be tough to make it in this world, so keep a poker face, meaning never show emotion. It's sad but that's the way most of us as men grew up. As I've journeyed through life and experienced countless situations, I now know that this kind of thinking is primitive and ignorant. I can recall as I was growing up my father really didn't talk with me much. He told me things, but never really asked me about my feelings. Maybe it was because he was too drunk to ask me how I was feeling, or maybe it was because he was taught not to talk about his feelings as a man. Not only did I want to talk with my father about my feelings, but I also wanted to know how he was feeling. I figured out, of all the people I knew, he would understand me more because I was his son.

I believe that when you know your child's likes and dislikes, fears, and dreams, this brings you closer together. This includes children talking to parents about their feelings and vice versa. Yes, you, Dad, also share your feelings! This type of healthy dialogue should occur continuously as it can help your child to understand the current situation concerning your incarceration. Once a proper understanding is established then can come acceptance and healthy adjustment. Through this experience, I've witnessed the stress of my having been locked up affect my son in different ways. Mainly it was hard for him to understand why I was not there with him. So I tried to remember to ask him how he felt every single time I was able to talk to him by phone or visit with him face-to-face.

Unfortunately, my son started to do as most males do and hide his feelings. Since we weren't able to talk to each other regularly on a one-on-one basis, I had to consider he may have felt embarrassed about disclosing his feelings to me with others present. Most of the time, I had to coax it out of him, and quietly cajole or gently tease him to talk about how he's feeling. I developed a tactic called bathroom break to get my probing questions in so Hakeem would not be put on the spot and feel self-conscious during our visits.

Whenever his mother or grandmother would go to the

bathroom or vending machine, I would use these short time frames to find out some of the things that may have been bothering my son. Some prisons have an outside court yard or a playroom for children that you can use and have a little more one-on-one privacy. This extra privacy is often just enough to make your child feel comfortable enough to open up to you.

You shouldn't confuse the joy your child is expressing during your visit as a sign that everything is okay back at home or school, or with the fact that you're here and their there. Yes, your child is happy to see you, but s/he may still be feeling some emotional pain due to your incarceration or even entirely something else altogether. It's important to remember that your incarceration is an unnatural occurrence in you and your child's relationship, so it's guaranteed there will be pain, anger, and resentment. For me it was painful just to wake up every day away from my child, so imagine how a kid feels. I was taught that talking about why you are feeling pain and the cause of it is the best way to take the sting out of it. Many incarcerated fathers may not know how to communicate or may have forgotten how due to the anti-social nature of life in prison.

From my experience, it's best to start off asking small questions like, how are you doing in school? Or, what kind of things do you do when you're home? You can also ask about any new places your children may have gone to or any new things they may have done. If they are into any sports activities, music, video games and such, you should be sure to use these as appetizers before getting into deeper topics dealing with emotions.

Young children lack tools essential to properly express themselves so it may be hard for them to talk about things that may be bothering them. It's hard to gauge how open a child may be when it comes to opening up about their feelings. Children may also convey their pain through their drawings or by telling you stories about someone else; this gives them a greater sense of control over an uncontrollable situation. It gives the child a feeling of ownership, and thereby, confidence to express their emotions easier. Once you feel confident your child is comfortable, throw in a serious question in between your warm up questions.

These questions can range from a number of topics, depending on the age of your child. There are some questions I refer to as universal questions, because it doesn't matter your child's age or gender. These questions are geared toward feelings the child has about you being in prison, or maybe about the current relationship Mom is in and how the new boyfriend or husband relates to your child. Drawing a smiley face and a mean face and asking your child to point to the one that reminds him of the new guy, can speak volumes without putting your child on the spot. You can also ask your child if s/he is bothered by anyone, for example, adults or other children asking your son or daughter to do or preform actions that they feel uncomfortable doing.

During my incarceration I encountered a situation wherein I found out my son was being physically abused and bullied by another family member outside of my immediate family. When I was told what happened to my son, I thought I was having a heart attack; I actually felt intense pain in my chest and I couldn't breathe. It was a nightmare hearing that my son was being hurt and I was not there to protect him. When my son came to visit me that week I didn't say much at first, I just held him for a while. Once I suppressed the lump in my throat, I told Hakeem that if he ever wanted to talk to me about anything he could. I explained to him that I'd never be mad at him, no matter what he told me. I found out later that the statement I made about me never being mad at him about anything he ever told me, had stuck in his head. As soon as Hakeem got home, he told his mother what I said.

It is important to build a bond with your children in order for them to trust you. And the key to your children trusting you is to make them feel comfortable and allow them to open up. But for me, the difficult time was yet to come. I still had to talk to my son about what had happened to him. To be honest, I'm not the best when it comes to talking about feelings. In this case I had no other option but to discuss the incident with my son because it is my duty to give him comfort and protection. Truthfully, I was embarrassed, but also it was painful for me thinking about what my son had been through. I also felt guilty because I had not been there to protect him.

Two visits came and went and I still hadn't mustered the courage to talk with my son about the incident. Finally on our fourth visit I felt I had the opportunity I needed to talk with him. He and I were playing a game of catch in the playroom for visiting children, and all of the other kids had left, which is something rare. I told my son that we should take a break from our game of catch, so we could talk for a minute. We sat down together on the floor, and then I explained that what had happened to him wasn't his fault, and I said that the person was wrong for what they did to him.

Then I told him if anyone ever tried to hurt him or make him do something he's not comfortable with or that he doesn't want to do, that he should right away tell me, or his mother or grandmother. I then explained that it is my job to protect him, and that he shouldn't keep any secrets from me. I told him it's okay to feel a little nervous or embarrassed, but he should always tell me when something or someone is bothering him. I still wanted to dig a little deeper, so I asked him how he was feeling and whether that person had tried to do any more bad things to him. He replied "no", and to my relief the incident was resolved.

Almost a year and a half had passed and thank God it hadn't happened again, but I still asked my son every chance I got if anyone is bothering him or has tried to hurt him.

For those fathers who are not able to visit with their children or communicate by phone, the next option is written letters. Even if your child is unable to read, there is most likely someone in the household who can read your letter privately to your son or daughter. I wrote to my son every week even though I visited with him once or twice a month. I also made sure to call him twice a month to help our communication grow further. Many times I forget the things I wanted to say to him or discuss during our visits or phone conversations.

Writing to my son gave me a chance to encapsulate all the things I'd forgotten. And it also gave my son reading practice which, I hope, will pay off in the future when he's taking his S.A.T.'s for college. I know that everyone's situation is different, and if you and your child's mother are not on the best terms then you may want to mail your letters to a family member's house. Preferably you can arrange this with one who has a lot of direct contact and interaction with your children, either a grandmother, grandfather, aunt, uncle, brother, sister, or any trusted person in your life willing to assist you.

Don't worry too much about the length of the letter; the most important thing is to let your children know that you love them. Pictures are a great way to communicate even though there are no words to read. A picture itself say's that s/he is on your mind. If you are an artist then this is something you can do with ease. I am not the best when it comes to drawing, so I would buy artwork from the local prison artists.

During my 70 month sentence I probably spent about $300 buying artwork to send to my son, daughter and my younger siblings, and nephews and neice. The goal is to continually keep your presence felt by your child. Communication keeps your memory alive. So don't become discouraged when you run into stumbling blocks. Just do your best to find another route. Don't become selfish and use the excuse that your child doesn't need to hear from you, or get caught up in the blame game of your children's mother not bringing your kids to see you or accepting your phone calls so you can talk with them. In the end your child will suffer by not hearing from you. So, communicate through an means at your disposal!

Chapter 6: PARENTING POINTS

- Create a budget with any finances you receive. If possible, dedicate a portion for child support.
- Communicate through all means at your disposal.
- Be a good listener.
- Be patient with your child when asking difficult questions.
- Don't be afraid to ask difficult questions.
- Always remind your child/children you are always available to listen and not judge.
- Encourage them to write to you, this a good way for them to express their feelings without feeling they are being put on the spot.

Chapter Seven

Just One Hour Away

IT HAD BEEN THREE YEARS since my incarceration began. As soon as I reached the 36-month mark, which was the amount of time left on my sentence, I was classified by my institution counselor as minimum custody. A few days later I was woken up before breakfast which is about 6:30 a.m., and was told to roll up my property. Wondering what trouble I might encounter at the next facility, I said to my cellmate, "I'll probably be seeing you soon." I transported all of my property to Receiving & Delivery which is where you go when you're leaving the institution or coming in. With all my property in tow I was escorted across the parking lot to the minimum custody unit. It felt really strange not being confined to four 20-foot walls that surrounded the recreation yard on the unit I was housed in.

For my first three years, the only thing I could see when I went outside was the sky. As I walked across to the minimum custody unit, I gazed across the landscape taking in the Eastern Oregon desert. Once in the minimum custody unit I knew immediately I wouldn't last very long there. For one thing, going from three years of living in a cell, to a dormitory style setting was a hard adjustment for me. You see, I went from a reasonable amount of privacy and few variables, to no privacy and too many variables.

The one thing that gave comfort was finding out that the minimum custody unit had its own visiting room. After some inquiring about the visiting room, I found out that it was ridiculously small. Add to that the fact that I had to live in an open dorm with 63 other people with whom I had to share a bathroom, showers, and living space, and you can imagine why this put me in a very irritable mood.

A week later my mother brought Hakeem to visit me along with my younger brother and sister. In order to get to the visiting room, we had to leave the minimum unit and walk through the parking lot to a separate building where minimum visiting was. I walked into the visiting room and was shocked by how small it was. They say never believe rumors, but the rumors were true. It was half the size of the visiting room over on the maximum side which I had become accustomed to for the last three years.

The officer pointed me in the direction of my family; I rounded the corner and my jaw dropped. I said to myself this can't be real. They had my family sitting in a cubby hole. The area was no more than four feet wide by four feet long, with brick walls on either side which served as a partition. Until my son leapt into my arms, I was distracted by this appalling scene. I hugged Hakeem tightly and kissed him on his soft cheek and told him how much I had missed him.

I put my son down and hugged the rest of my family. After we finished hugging we all sat down and began talking about me being in minimum custody, and how it felt to have more freedom. For some reason I couldn't take my mind off of the virtual closet we were sitting in—audaciously referred to as a visiting room.

One of the great things I love about my family is that we know how to make the best out of any situation. My son pulled out a board game and we began to play while I simultaneously talked with my mother. Before I knew it, the visit was coming to a close. Then came the part we all dreaded—saying goodbye. My family left the building and headed to the parking lot. After I and other inmates were patted down by the visiting officer we were marched out by our escort.

Walking through the parking lot toward the minimum unit I was able to wave good-bye and say I love you to my family as they were piling into my Mom's minivan. I think it was good for my son to see me walk freely through the parking lot. Some of the smallest things can make a difference, like a son being able to see his Dad in a semi-free condition, outside of tall brick walls and razor wire. I can honestly say that being in prison has made me appreciate the small things in life.

Sorry to say, the officers were to petty for me to make it in the minimum unit. Three weeks later I was sent to the hole for disobeying a direct order and showing disrespect to an officer. This was my third time being sent to the hole during my stay at this prison, so it really wasn't a big deal to me. The hole— known formally as the Administrative Segregation Unit—was a unit consisting of single cells, where inmates are locked up 23 hours a day. Inmates receive a shower every three days, recreation time and one 20-minute phone call, which must all be done within one hour.

I would rather have been back in a cell, and having visits in a semi-decent visiting room. So, my infraction was actually a blessing. I spent seven days in the hole. Once I was released, I had seven days' loss of privileges. This meant I could only leave my cell to eat, shower, and go to visits, the infirmary, and religious services.

Many people may not know that every prison across the U.S. is racially divided. When I was released from the hole I was put in a cell with a White inmate, which made my situation more uncomfortable. I noticed the lightning bolt tattoo on his neck signifying the Aryan brotherhood. We made eye contact as he

Just One Hour Away   89

walked out of the cell. My intention was to convey to him in one steely look that he better not say anything stupid about race to me.

Before I unpacked my property, my new cellmate was already in the Sergeant's office. I was then called to his office and he told me I would be moving upstairs because my current cellmate and I weren't compatible. You damn right! I was moved to another cell with a Hispanic guy who didn't speak English, which was fine with me. And I didn't speak Spanish which meant we didn't have to talk. That night I put in a cell move request, to cell-up with a Non-White, Non-Spanish-speaking person, a/k/a a Black guy.

In order to be scored minimum custody, an inmate's institutional point level has to be below 250. Your institution counselor determines this by using a number of variables. Anyone who receives a misconduct report increases his point level anywhere from five to seven points. The misconduct report that sent me to the hole now scored me at a 255. My third day out of the hole I was surprised to be woken up at six in the morning over the intercom in my cell: "Bossman roll up!" I asked the officer where I was going, but he said he didn't know and that I was just to report to R & D which is the acronym they use to refer to the intake and transport area.

All I could think was that I was probably going back to the minimum facility outside the gate, and truthfully, I didn't want to go back there. I entered R & D with my property and was told by the officer to put on a white jumpsuit. This meant I was being transported to another facility. As the officer was tagging my property I noticed the tag said Columbia River which was a minimum facility in Portland. My heart began to race from the excitement of being only 15 minutes away from my family.

Five of us were loaded onto a transport bus which we referred to as the gray goose, due to its length, size, and color. It was a three-hour ride from Umatilla to Portland and usually I'd sleep the whole ride through, but this time I wanted to enjoy the scenery. It had been three long hard years since I had seen mountains and rivers. During the ride, all I could think about was how I would be able to see my son and family all the time. This transfer also gave me the feeling that I was about to see better days. Even though I still had two years and five months and some change it still felt like I was almost home. After a long and stiff three-hour ride, we finally

arrived in Portland. I thought how I couldn't wait to get this black

box off my wrist. The black box was a device that was invented by a

former inmate.

The black box was, basically, just a box that was about four

inches in length with a handcuff coming out of each side of the box.

The box was put on each inmate with the right hand in the top cuff

pointing left, and the left hand in the bottom cuff pointing right.

Any amount of time wearing one of those black boxes is torture, let

alone three hours on a bus.

As we approached our destination, it gave me a good feeling

driving through the city and seeing familiar landmarks, streets, and

buildings. On arrival, I wished the ride was just a little bit longer,

but the gates to Columbia River Correctional Institution opened

and we pulled in. Out of the five total inmates on the bus, one other

inmate and I were the only two leaving the bus. The transport

officers unshackled us and walked us in to R & D. Then they turned

and left to continue their transport, heading toward institutions in

Salem, Oregon's capital.

I was at Columbia River for four days when the rug was pulled out from beneath my feet. Once again, I was awoken at 6:00 a.m., and told to roll up my property. I headed down to Intake with my belongings and put on another white jumpsuit and was loaded onto another transport bus. I found out quickly that my destination was Oregon State Penitentiary also known as "The Walls" because it is surrounded by 60-foot high concrete walls.

Oregon State Penitentiary was located in the city of Salem which is about a 45 minute to an hour from Portland, give or take. At first, I was really upset about being moved from Columbia River but I thought to myself that anything is better than being at Two Rivers Correctional Institution, which is three long hours away. The ride from Portland to Salem is pretty boring—just a few farms and open fields along the highway. During the ride, I heard a few guys talking about how big the visiting room is at O.S.P., and how it had an outside area and a playroom for children. After doing three years out east in Umatilla, Oregon where the officers are not used to dealing with African American culture, it was a burden off of my shoulders to be at a prison where the African American population is a lot more prominent.

When we finally arrived at Oregon State Penitentiary, I thought it looked old and decrepit, dark like those dreary prisons in movies. After being herded into Intake, we dressed down and then listened carefully to the Intake Sergeant as he gave his welcome to Oregon State Penitentiary speech. The rest of the new arrivals and I were directed to the office of the housing assignment officer. Once we arrived we were given a bedroll that consisted of two sheets, two towels, two blankets, and one pillow case. Then we were given our cell numbers and told which block they were located in.

After putting my things away and introducing myself to my new cellmate, I headed straight to the yard. All 25 phone booths are in the yard; I stepped into a booth and dialed my mother's number. Before I could even enter my pin number a brother approached me, and I asked him, What's up? With an icy stare looking dead into my eyes, he told me all the inmates were on phone strike, and anyone who used the phone would suffer consequences and repercussions from members of their race. This meant Blacks would discipline Blacks, Whites would discipline Whites, Hispanics would discipline

Hispanics, Native Americans would discipline Native Americans, and Asians would discipline Asians.

Then to make matters worse, the Black inmate also told me that the inmates were also on a canteen strike. Inside my head I screamed, Damn it! I had just spent seven days in the hole, was on seven days of loss of privileges and I'd been transported twice in less than a week's time. My hygiene items were just about gone and food-wise I was down to a few packs of Top Ramen noodles. I swear I was really getting pissed off with all this bullshit. Luckily, I knew a few brothers whom I had done time with at Two Rivers who understood my situation. They gave me the necessary items I needed to make it through the strike, because at this point all I could do was pray it was over soon.

That night after getting adjusted, I wrote my mother a letter letting her know that I had been transferred again and I would probably be there for a while. The prison where I was now housed was very old, in fact it was the first prison built in Oregon in 1859. Oregon State Penitentiary is the second largest prison in the state housing about 2,000 inmates. There are four major housing blocks each consisting of five tiers with 20 cells on either side. The cells were so small I could literally spread my arms and touch the walls at the same time. Mind you, I am only 5'8" ½ inches, so standing in that cell was just like standing in a hallway closet. There were no doors on the cells like Two Rivers Correctional facility.

As this is the oldest prison in Oregon, this was all old school—the real deal. Steel bars were all that enclosed me plus three cement walls. This meant no privacy and the temperature was basically whatever the weather happed to be like. I found out quick that prisoners do a lot of cell time here. In some ways, it was a good thing, because it was an opportunity to focus on myself and forget about the daily prison politics between prisoners, prison gangs, and correction officers. But being confined to such a small space for up to eighteen hours a day could also drive a person crazy. Nevertheless, I was closer to my family and that was worth any sacrifice.

During my ride from Columbia River Correctional Institution I heard a few guys talking about the visiting room. I did some inquiring to make sure that what I heard was true. The visiting room had a play room for children where the inmates and families could go to spend time during visits. This was the best news I'd had since I arrived at this raggedy, depressing prison.

Seven days later the strike was over and as soon as I hit the yard I rushed to the pay phone and called my mother. Once the recorded phone message ended I immediately heard the joy and relief in my mother's voice when she said hello. After I finished giving her the run down about the strike and how I was adjusting to my new environment, I asked her how the family was and when she had last seen my son, and how he was doing. I told her about the visiting room and how I was excited about being able to play with my son in the playroom of this facility. We talked a bit more and she told me she planned to visit me the coming weekend with my son. I thanked her for taking the time out to bring Hakeem to visit and how we both loved her dearly.

During that week, I saw my institution counselor who told me that I would have to remain at O.S.P. for one year before I could be classed as minimum again. He explained to me the main reason I had to wait so long was because of my age and some other criteria I fell into. I wanted to get upset but I knew it wouldn't have made a difference. My main concern was staying out of trouble and not going to the hole. This institution was one of the most violent in the state. You were guaranteed to see a fight every day. I had been doing time for three years now so I knew how to stay away from the bullshit that will get you caught up on the wrong side of right. As they say, "Just do your number."

It had been about a month since I had last seen my son, so just thinking about our upcoming visit put me in a joyous state. My week went by rabbit fast and suddenly Friday was here and I knew that I should be getting a visit the next day. When my name was called next morning for a visit I was on the yard so I had to hurry back to my cell to get dressed. I walked into the visiting room and made my way to where my family was sitting. It was the usual bunch, my mom, Hakeem, and my younger brother and sister.

Hakeem rocketed into the air as if he had springs on his feet, calling out Daddy, Daddy. I grabbed him out of the air and hugged him and kissed his cheek while hugging the rest of my family. Before I could sit down, my son blurted out, "Dad, can we go in the play room?" I cracked a big smile and told him of course we could, and then he, my baby sister, and I headed off to the playroom. My younger brother couldn't come in the playroom because he was over eight-years-old so he and my mother played cards at our table.

Once in the playroom we found a soccer ball and started up a game. This was one of Hakeem's favorite sports and at that time he was in his second season of soccer playing for a local team in his neighborhood. Within 15 minutes I was tired so we switched up to a game of basketball which was also one of his favorite sports. We made a make shift basketball hoop and started our game. And now of course I had to let my son win, not because he was a kid, but just because he was a sore loser at that age, and I wanted very much to keep him happy.

After a couple rounds of B-ball we took a break and went back into the visiting area and had some juice and chips. I took this time to talk with my mother and brother about how he was doing in school and how work was going for her. Once we finished our short break, my son and I went back into the playroom, but my little sister said she was tired so she sat out the second round. We went through another game of let's get Daddy out of breath. And before I knew it our visiting time was over. This time it wasn't so bad because this was the best visit I had had since my incarceration.

As my family was leaving, I could tell by the smile on Hakeem's face that he also had had a good time and he wasn't as sad as he normally was after our visits during the past three years. Even though I was still in prison this was a positive experience which I hoped would erase some of the dark memories of my incarceration. I remember thinking, I guess this place isn't so bad after all.

Chapter 7: PARENTING POINTS

- Focus on making the best of your visit, regardless of the conditions of the prison visiting area. Focus on delighting your child.

- When arriving at any new facility, inquire about the visiting area and the rules. Find ways to use working within the rules to your advantage to ensure a positive visit for yourself and for your child.

- If your prison has a playroom, outside courtyard, or other space for one-on-one time with your children, grab the opportunity to give them personal interaction time.

- The more time you can spend with your child the better. Usually when you transition to minimum custody you are allowed more privileges; this may enable you and your visitors to experience a less stressful visit.

Thank God for Grandmothers

TO BE AN EXCELLENT FATHER to your child, you don't have

to have a family that gets along. Yet, it sure helps. I am very

fortunate that my mother and my son's mother have a healthy

relationship with each other. This has played a critical part in the

relationship between my son and me, especially during the time I

was incarcerated. The love that these women possess for Hakeem

has always remained unconditional. My son loves his grandmother

and, after his mother and me, Nana is the next most important person in his life.

Since the birth of Hakeem, my mother has been there, and when I say since his birth I mean it literally. My mother was in the birthing room at the hospital while my son was being born and she coached his mother through the labor process.

I have a close-knit family and, since I can remember, it has always been that way, we were always taught to support one another. Before my mother moved to Portland, Oregon from Boston, Massachusetts, every Sunday we would go to my grandmother's house for dinner. There, all my family members would meet to eat great Southern food, mingle, and discuss family issues.

In the Portland, Oregon hospital delivery room, when my son's tiny body came into this world, I was the first to hold him, before passing him to his mother. And the third face my son saw, was none other than -My Mother-? Nana! And instantly the bond between them formed. Now, there are grandmothers out there who see grandchildren on a see-you-when-I-see-you basis. Let me assure you my mother is not one of these grandmothers; she consistently demanded her time with her grandson.

I can say with certainty that for the first three and a half years of Hakeem's life he saw his grandmother no less than once a week. You may think I am stretching the truth, but once my son entered my mother's house I had no more parental rights. If my son even cried the first thing I heard was, "What are you doing to my baby?" I recall numerous times when my mother and I had it out about me being too hard on my son when he pitched a normal kid fit. In the end she always won, while snatching my crying son out of my arms with the final decree, "This is my house and that's my grandson." Eventually my son realized that his grandmother would save him whenever he didn't want to do what I asked of him. It got to the point that when it was time to leave my mother's house, my son would throw a tantrum—kicking, screaming, and sometimes even throwing things.

Being that my son was the first grandchild among her children my beloved mother could not show her love any other way than her classic tour de force granny act. My son would also spend weekends at my mother's during my incarceration and throughout my near-six years in prison.

In her defense, my Mom continually showed my son a picture of me, talked to him about me, and always reminded him your Daddy loves you during my incarceration. I think my mother may feel guilty about me not having the best relationship with my father. Or that her past husbands were not the best role models to me during my formative years. Possibly she felt compelled now to do everything in her power to make sure my son and I stayed close— albeit while she ruled the roost with her soft-gloved iron fist. Truthfully, without my mother doing 100% of the transportation bringing my son back forth to see me, I doubt the bond my son and I have today would be as strong. Thank you, mom!

Before I was incarcerated, my son and I had a very close relationship, but experience showed me I cannot stop the change bought on by the hands of time. With my son still very young I was afraid that a barrier would develop between us since we could only see each other once a month—a barrier that would take as long to tear down as it took to build up.

When children are young and their parents go through a divorce or separation it is critical that they receive constant attention and communication from both parents. That's what my mother provided for my son and me. By her continuously speaking on my behalf, Hakeem was able to continue to feel my presence. It would have been nice if Hakeem's mother could have brought my son to see me more, but things don't always work out the way we would like. I really didn't expect much from her at this time since she was in another relationship with someone who still thought she had feelings for me.

I feel she was torn between doing right by her child and trying to make her boyfriend happy and not jealous. More often than not when the mother of your child starts a new relationship she sometimes is given a guilt trip by her significant other for still having contact with their child's father, especially when the father of the child is incarcerated. The new boyfriend or husband usually feels that he is the one responsible for his new family, and memories of any past relationships she's had must be extinguished. Most men don't want their current wife or girlfriend having any contact with the ex, let alone an ex who's deemed a criminal. With children involved, it sometimes makes the situation a little more difficult due to the inevitable contact that parents who are no longer together have and must maintain on a positive level for their child's sake. And, unfortunately this puts the new husband or boyfriend in a constant defensive mode, especially if he is insecure.

Such interference can cause a lot of damage to parents continuing a healthy relationship with one another and with their children; once the communication is interrupted or severed, the child will most definitely suffer. My mother was that voice for me when I needed to speak with Hakeem's mother. If I was lucky I could sometimes catch Hakeem's mother at my mom's house when I called. I would always try and keep the conversations general, only inquiring about my son, his health, well-being, and how he was adjusting to me being in prison.

If it wasn't for my son being at my mother's house so often, I never would have been able to speak with my ex at all. Whenever my Mom would bring my son to see me, she would always make it a field trip experience. She would put a great lunch together so my brother, sister, and son could have something to eat after the visit with me. They would sometimes go to parks, lakes, and even fishing where my son once caught a six-pound Pike Minnow.

Once, my mother even arranged to have herself, her husband, and my son flown in a small Cessna airplane to come visit me. One thing I really appreciated is that whenever my mother would bring my son to see me, she would never use the word jail when she told him where they were headed. All she would say is, "We are going to visit your Dad." Now, of course he knew I was in prison, but my mother would never say those words. Another good thing about grandmothers who are involved in their grandchildren's lives is that they stay up on the current events surrounding or affecting the children's lives.

Whenever I would call my mother's house she would update me on Hakeem's activities, health, education, and anything else I needed to know as his parent. This is the fuel I would use to get my son to open up when I spoke with him, be it by phone or a visit face-to-face. I think this gave him a sense of ease to know that even though he and I didn't see each other every day, I still knew what was going on in his life. It's hard enough not seeing your children daily, so being able to talk to them about their fears, likes, dislikes, or anything else going on in their life, reassures that you have not totally abandoned the family. My mother and son have a great relationship and that's a big help, because it allows him to still feel my presence through her.

For any incarcerated father reading this book, if you have the option to keep your children's grandmother or grandfather in their lives you should do so. If nothing else, an extra set of caring eyes is a good way to stay updated on your child's daily activities and general well-being. Hakeem's mother seldom remembered to send pictures, so my mother would make sure to attend most of Hakeem's major events—graduations, sporting events, plays, or anything she warranted deserved a photo she would shoot. I'm pretty sure most incarcerated fathers feel the same way I felt about photos of my child; they're worth more than gold. Whenever I received a photo of my son at a special event I could always picture myself there with him and it also reminded me painfully how important it is to be available for your child.

I am glad my mother is the way she is with stern, deep-rooted morals, and a strong character. And I know if anything happened to

Hakeem's mother, my son would be in good hands with his grandmother. One of the biggest offerings of help from my mother was the positive outlook that she exuded during my incarceration. Most importantly, this helped my son keep a positive attitude. To my mind, a father's choice to maintain a positive outlook during incarceration is essential to helping your children remain positive during your incarceration.

Number one is communication because with that key ingredient you can show your child many types of examples of how you are staying positive. Whether it's verbal, written, face-to-face, or by phone, communication is the integral key in keeping the bond healthy and strong between you and your child. It's not only about keeping grandmothers involved, but all family members because you never know whom you may need to bring your child to see you and constantly keep you updated on your children's lives. It's best to be prepared by seeding any and all opportunities to create positive relationships with willing and available family members and friends.

Chapter 8: PARENTING POINTS

+ Reach out to as many family members and friends as you can think of.

+ If possible, establish a circle of support to help keep you involved in and updated about your child's schooling, activities, health, and over-all wellbeing.

+ Remember to continuously thank and show your appreciation to all those who are sacrificing their time and finances to assist you.

+ If the mother of your child or children is or has started a new relationship, it helps to respect her boundaries. Keep your conversationsn and your interactions revolving solely around your child/children. Ask continually how you can assist, suggest any way that may help ease the burden of her having to parent without you your day-to-day presence.

Stress Management

BEING LOCKED AWAY IS TRULY beyond stressful. Just the fact of waking up every day in a depressing and violent environment is enough to make a person lose their mind. Believe me when I say this, I've seen it happen on more than one occasion. Going from being a free man and being involved in your child's life on a daily basis, to basic communication and your physical presence being stripped from your child and family is just one cause of stress. Factor in that your prison location may change every few weeks or months, and in some cases an inmate may get shipped so far from his family that they are not able to visit him at all.

For a lot of incarcerated fathers, myself included, contact and communication with my son kept me from losing my temper and thinking irrationally when it came to stressful situations. When a person is incarcerated and stripped of his freedom and dignity with a long sentence looming ahead, life becomes more intensified. Minor changes like not eating at the time the meal schedule stated have, in some cases, turned into full scale riots.

The hardest thing for me was controlling my temper and walking away from potential physical confrontations. When two inmates are caught fighting they are confined to the Administrative Segregation, aka the hole for a minimum of 30 days and up to a maximum 180 days. When an inmate receives a visit while doing time in the hole, it is behind glass and he is confined by wrist, ankle, and belly chains on his way to his visit, that was the best-case scenario. The worst-case scenario was when inmates end up fighting in a heavily populated area, like the chow hall or the recreation yard, and it leads to a charge of inciting a riot; fights of this nature guarantee a straight shot to the Intense Management Unit, which can range with a sentencing at a minimum of one year up to the maximum of five years.

The only fight worse than this would be if you injured a person while fighting, caused one of their bones to break, or used a weapon. This would bring a charge by the state police. If convicted of assault in the 2nd degree an inmate can get a year or more added to his sentence.

Since I was fortunate enough to have contact with my son, this helped deter me from getting into a lot of trouble, and kept me from getting consumed by the stress and depression that life in prison causes. Most men who are in prison are used to expressing themselves with violence when confronted with a stressful situation; this makes fights and other violent attacks an everyday occurrence in prison. To shield oneself it is important to remain positive; the best way I found to do that was by keeping positive activities in my daily schedule, so I had things to look forward to. But the best tonic in my opinion has proven to be prayer.

I come from a very religious and God conscientious family. I can admit when I was free I didn't pray like I was supposed to or refrain from drugs and alcohol. When all you have is time on your hands you can do two things: Waste it or use it to your advantage. So, I decided this was an opportune time for me to really figure out my strengths and weaknesses and what my purpose was in life.

Throughout my prison experience the thing that was most stressful for me was not being able to be with my son and family on a regular daily basis. What hurt the most? I was missing out on all the things that most of us as parents take for granted, like simple father and son activities, or going to his basketball and soccer games, teaching him how to be tough when he hurts himself, or teaching him how to ride his bike. Most of all, I was pained not being able to comfort him when he was in pain or hurting emotionally. These were the daily stresses I found to be hardest to deal with.

I know that these are the times when children really bond with their parents. It's our job as parents to give our children reassurance that we will be there when they need us. Being there to pick them up when they fall, or encouraging them to try harder when faced with a difficult trial.

When my son turned seven-years-old, I was hit with the worst case of stress yet, was when Hakeem's mother told me that my son had been physically and psychologically abused by one of her own family members. The whole time she was speaking, I was gasping for air; I just kept thinking that this wasn't real, that I must have misunderstood what she said. After she finished talking there was just silence for another minute or so. When I finally spoke, I asked her when this had occurred. To my surprise it had happened months before. This made me furious to know that someone had hurt my child and I wasn't told immediately.

All I wanted to know was why all this information had been kept from me. She explained that she and my mother had a talk and they came to the consensus that it would be best not to tell me immediately due to their fear of me going into a rage. Damn right it would have and damn right it did. I reminded her that Hakeem was my son also and I should have been the second to know after her.

After the phone conversation with Hakeem's mother I went back to my cell. At that point, my rage was so strong that I couldn't think straight. What I had just heard was worse than when the judge told me I was going to prison for 70 months and I would have to do every day of it. All I wanted to do at this point was see my son and tell him that I was there to protect him, and I wouldn't let anyone hurt him ever again.

No matter how much I wished and wanted, I could not be there to protect him, and this fueled my anger ever more. This is still hard for me to think about and it was even harder when I first found out. I had never dealt with a situation this serious and delicate in my life. In situations of this magnitude it is critical to try and keep anger and emotions in check. For the rest of the week I was very agitated, so I tried to stay in my cell as much as possible so as not to encounter or create any conflict with the prison guards or other inmates.

The only times I would leave my cell were to eat, shower, and work, then it was straight back to my cell. I constantly had the urge to beat the shit out of anyone convicted of a crime against children, and believe me, I had more than enough of those candidates in my block to choose from. As bad as I wanted to kick someone's ass, I knew that type of behavior would only make matters worse. The result would have been me sitting in the hole for about 40 days, visiting my son and family behind glass., in an orange jumpsuit talking through a two-way phone. I had a choice to either focus on being a better person for my son, or totally lose it and get sent to the hole.

So, I prayed hard asking the Creator to give me the strength to stay focused and control my anger. I have always had trouble controlling my anger, so this was a true test for me. I was lucky to have a good friend named Roo with whom I bonded over the years. I was able to talk to with him about what happened to my son and the anger I was feeling. Roo helped me to see that I was doing the right thing by not reacting violently, and helped me realize that what happened to my son wasn't my fault, and not to let the guilt of not being there to protect Hakeem eat me up inside.

I advise anyone who has a friend like Roo to confide in to do so rather than react impulsively with violence. Often times, inmates are stressed to the point that even the wind blowing in the wrong direction can cause them to snap and lose control; that always leads to making irrational decisions which, ultimately, only hurt the inmate. It's hard to talk about personal feelings in prison, as it is seen as a sign of weakness. In prison, the last thing you want to do is look vulnerable. Making bad decisions and letting anger take over will only make your situation worse. This will not only compound your stress but it will also lead to more emotional distress for your family and children being that they are now more concerned for your welfare.

Eventually, with time, I learned to choose deliberately to deal with stressful situations in a more positive manner—as new challenges, or puzzles I alone had to resolve. The first thing I had to do was understand that I could not control what went on outside of the prison walls, or even within them, for that matter; in fact, the only thing I could control was what was going through my own head and how I chose to react to it.

It's hard enough controlling life as an inmate when 95% of the time actions and movements are dictated by someone who views prisoners as less than human. Prison guards are often not sympathetic to the stress an inmate may be under and some go out of their way to add stress to inmates' daily lives in prison. Over time, I became a master of what's called rolling with the punches. This kind of mentality can have a positive and negative effect when adopted. The positive side is that it helps inmates cope with stressful situations. But on the negative side, they can end up building a hard shell around themselves which can be hard to break down; it can become harmful to their psyche, and short-circuit developing new relationships.

I know a lot of guys who have let their anger get the best of them, who then did something they wish they could take back. Sometimes you have to ask yourself, Do I want to be right or do I want to feel better? Being right isn't all it's cracked up to be, so sometimes it's better to go with the feel better. Most prisons offer some sort of anger management or stress management class that, in the long run, will make you feel better. My advice to anyone who is incarcerated and reading this book is to take advantage of any such class your institution has to offer.

Some people handle stress better than others. But no matter how long you're able to hold it in, you must find an outlet for it. When my stress level builds up and reaches the overload point I have a natural alarm that lets me know it's time to release it before it boils over. The first warning sign for me is when I find myself becoming easily irritated by small things, which spirals me downward into a foul mood. The second warning sign is when I find myself wanting to hit something or someone.

Lastly and this is my most telltale sign, is when my face breaks out in hives, like a rash. I have also found that meditating when I am stressed helps put me in a relaxed state. Whenever I am alone I close my eyes and take deep, slow breaths in through my nose and out through my mouth, counting to six each way. Once you start to feel relaxed, try and think of something positive that brings you joy for 17 seconds—like, an image of your child. Remarkably, 17 seconds is long enough to jar your attention and tip the scales, and then it's easier for you to choose to just chill out and smile.

And, even though it may sound like an oddball cliché that someone's Great Aunt Martha told you, baby, once you start smiling, your body takes over and releases happy hormones in your brain called endorphins. I also use working with weights as a way to relieve stress and release endorphins. On days when I am really feeling stressed, I try to work out with heavier weights. And when I feel I can't lift anymore due to muscle fatigue, I focus on the source of my anger or stress and try to push out a few more reps—channeling anger into positive energy is never an easy feat, but when accomplished it can bring you a great sense of peace. Stress build up can be very dangerous and can also lead to health problems.

So, my advice is not to let it build up. But, when it docs, try to find a positive outlet for it. In the long run, you will thank yourself. Remember a positive will always add to a positive and negatives always take away from positives. Math never lies.

Chapter 9: PARENTING POINTS

+ Find a way to channel negative energy it positive energy; update your joy list, exercise, pray, meditate, draw, play music, etc.

+ Always take into consideration that each of your actions may affect your child/children or family.

+ Find someone you feel comfortable confiding in. Attend anger management classes.

+ Identify your triggers. And isolate antidotes and solutions.

Chapter Ten
My New Daughter

DURING THE FIRST YEAR OF my incarceration Hakeem's mother divorced her husband of a one-year duration. During their marriage, they had a daughter and named her Kadijah. But due to her husband's infidelity they separated and he moved out of the state, leaving her with their barely one-year-old daughter. Throughout the process of the divorce, Hakeem's mother and I began communicating again. We first began writing letters to each other, then every Saturday she would go to my mother's house and wait for my weekly phone call. To my surprise, the tone of our conversations grew increasingly personal.

Eventually, Hakeem's mother made the three-hour trip with my mother to visit me. It had been about a year since I'd last seen Neisy. I will admit, at that time I still had feelings for the mother of my son. After about a month or so of constant correspondence and a second visit, we decided to explore the option of starting a relationship again. At that point, I was thrilled that we were going to be a family again.

But what I deliberately ignored was that relationships forged of loneliness tend not to last long. After about a month and a half of Neisy and I being back together, we realized that our year and a half apart had really taken both of us in different directions. Ultimately, we came to the decision to just be friends. I was crushed but we both knew that this was the right choice. I learned that good things can evolve into something vastly different than what you may have initially imagined.

It was unspoken, but I think we knew that she was looking for a shoulder to lean on while going through her divorce. Personally, I was just happy to have a woman say that she would support me emotionally through my next 58 months of a very lonely and depressing prison term. But the real icing on the cake for me was that she wasn't just any woman, she was the mother of my son and someone whom I was still in love with. We knew that being friends was safe, and we both wanted to protect our feelings and not hurt one another out of selfishness, so we left our fate in the hands of the Creator.

Gradually, I settled into our newfound friendship and it really wasn't as hard as I had imagined. To me, our friendship meant that there was hope we could become a couple again somewhere down the road. Seeing that we had a son together who was going on five-years-old, it was important for us to have, at least, a cordial relationship. In my mind's eye, building a true friendship was even better because I hoped it would help fix some of the mess I made a year and a half before we broke up.

As the years went by, Neisy and I became closer and closer as friends, and there were still unspoken feelings on both ends. Sad to say, she started another relationship, but we still kept an open line of communication through phone calls, letters, and visits every now and again which helped to strengthen our bond as friends and co-parents.

I have a loving family, and we were always taught to love and nurture children no matter what. Whenever my son would go over to my mother's house his sister would also go. She was treated just like a granddaughter by my mother, and a niece by my brothers and sisters. During the years of my incarceration, I tried to provide for my son the best I could, buying him school clothes at the beginning of the school year, presents on his birthdays, and any other occasion my finances would allow. For the past five years, Kadijah had watched her brother Hakeem's father provide for him. She also had learned a lot about me through my family, so she kind of knew me in an indirect way.

The fourth year into my sentence I decided to write my son a letter once a week. At that time, he was in second grade, so his reading skills were good. Therefore, I asked about specifics in his life and school. I told him how much I loved him and that I was proud of him always. I absolutely never chose to share with my child any of the depressing, negative experiences of prison life. Instead, I chose to focus on reinforcing my son's good qualities.

That year, Hakeem won an award or two for best reader in his class. I figured writing letters would be a great way to keep my presence strong in his life, and also give him good reading practice. After a year of writing letters to my son, I received a shocking request from his sister as I was talking to her on the phone one day.

To put in context little Kadijah's request, at that time, I would talk to Hakeem's sister pretty often when I would call to talk with my son. Whenever I spoke with my son, his sister would want to say hi and we'd talk for a minute. On this particular day, I was just finishing up my conversation with my son when he told me his sister wanted to say hi to me. I told Hakeem I loved him and then he put Kadijah on the phone. We talked about how she was doing and how she liked her school. I had talked to her many times in the past, but today her voice sounded different. Today she had a sense of urgency in her tone but with a hint of excitement.

Then, without warning, she asked me how come I don't write her letters like I do to my son? I didn't really have an answer to her question so I asked her if she would like me to write her letters also, and she said that yes she would like that. So, from that day forward, when I wrote my son his weekly letter, I would write one for his sister also and stuff it in the same envelope

Three to four months had passed since I began sending Kadijah letters. During one of my weekly phone calls while Kadijah and I were talking, she asked me a question that caught me completely off guard: "Who are you to me?" she asked. I paused. Who was I to her? Stopped in my tracks by a small girl, I searched desperately for an answer to give her. I fell silent, deep in thought. Kadijah became impatient with me and asked, "Are you my uncle?" I said I didn't know.

Since I couldn't find an answer to her first question, I asked her what she wanted me to be to her. She said she also didn't know. All of a sudden, a little voice in my head told me to ask her if she wanted me to be her Dad. I believe this was just my parental intuition understanding that she also wanted a father no matter the circumstance, since her own father had abandoned his responsibilities when she was one year's old. Even with me being incarcerated, she still was able to see the love Hakeem received from me. So, when I asked her, she immediately and without hesitation said that yes she wanted me to be her Dad.

Now mind you, she and I had never met face-to-face. I knew what my next reply to this innocent child had to be, and I agreed I would be her Dad. Before I had a chance to say anything more, the phone recording announced that we were at the one-minute mark. I told Kadijah I loved her and we reluctantly said our good-byes and I hung up.

Later on, that week I called Hakeem's mother and told her the questions her daughter had asked me. She asked me what I said, and I said that I told Kadijah I would be her Dad. She then told me that recently Kadijah had called Neisy's current boyfriend Daddy, and he had responded by giving her a cold look. From that day forth, Kadijah never called him Daddy again. My ex- and I then discussed how she wasn't comfortable with the idea of me adopting her daughter.

Not because I wasn't a good father, but because Neisy felt that it might obligate my ex to be with me in a relationship. I explained to her that she had no reason to be concerned about that. I decided to adopt Kadijah because I felt it was what God wanted me to do, and that Neisy didn't owe me anything in the form of a relationship. I told Neisy I had given this issue a lot of deep thought, and my decision was solely for the benefit of Kadijah. I then explained that once I was released and resumed my full parental duties with Hakeem it would be hard for me to send him home with new clothes or toys while sending nothing to Kadijah.

Forget the way I would feel. Most importantly, how would Kadijah feel? Or if I were taking Hakeem somewhere and Kadijah asked to come, how could I tell her no? I have been a mean person before but I couldn't be that mean, and deny this little girl a father figure. Neisy and I then talked about the religion I practice which tells me that I am obligated and commanded by God to take care of the orphan and wayfarer. In my eyes, Kadijah was an orphan because her biological father had abandoned her four years earlier; he'd had no contact with her since he walked out on them for another woman.

I told Neisy Kadijah deserved a father and she shouldn't have to wait until her mother found the right guy who was willing to accept

Kadijah as his own. I felt I was in the best position to take on this responsibility because Neisy and I already had a son together. Secondly, Kadijah and I had developed a bond, and lastly, my family had accepted Neisy's daughter as a granddaughter and niece. Most pivotal, Kadijah saw all the love Hakeem got from me as a father, so even though I was in prison, I was still seen as a positive role model.

At the end of our conversation, Neisy agreed to think about it, but until she made her final decision we decided to leave the situation as it was.

A week had gone by since I accepted the role of father to Kadijah. During one of my weekly calls to Hakeem and Kadijah, Kadijah posed her third question to me, "When am I going to come see you?" I responded with soon but the truth was, until her mother got a Notary Public to notarize the special form for children to visit in a prison, I would have to keep telling my new daughter that she would see me soon every time she asked.

When Kadijah and I finished talking, Hakeem got on the phone. I told him how he was a good brother by sharing me with his sister and letting me be her Dad, too. After we finished our conversation, his mother got on the phone. Immediately, I asked her why it was taking so long to get the visitation form notarized. She gave me a lame excuse saying that she just hadn't had a chance to go to the Notary Public, but by her tone I could tell she was still having mixed feelings about me being Kadijah's father.

I reassured her again that my adopting Kadijah had nothing to do with the way I felt about Neisy, nor thoughts of us having a future relationship. Then she asked me how I would feel if she got married. I thought to myself, here we go again. So, I simply explained that we already have a child together who is biologically mine whom I take care of, so what difference did it make if I claimed her daughter as mine and treated her the same way I treat my son. If anything, it would work to her favor relative to a relationship with another man, seeing that I would be responsible for both children, providing for them 100% as a father. What man stepping into a relationship with a woman who has two children wouldn't want that?

Speaking from experience most men who enter a relationship with a woman would rather that the father of her child or children provide for them. A lot of relationships with children already in the mix don't work out because the current boyfriend or husband isn't willing to accept the child or children as his own. Or, to say it with brutal honesty, few men would want the responsibility of having to love and support children fathered by another man.

Suddenly out of left field, Neisy admitted she was scared that I might hurt Kadijah's feelings by building a relationship with her while I am in prison, but then abandon her when I get out, as an act of revenge for something Neisy did in our past for which I had felt betrayed. At the risk of sounding redundant, once again I reassured Neisy that what I was doing was for the sole benefit of Kadijah as a little human being alone in the world without a father. Secondly, Neisy knew me better than to think I would hurt an innocent child to get back at her for something she did far in the past, and for which I had already forgiven her.

It took a good twenty minutes for Neisy to express all her fears and concerns. Before our conversation ended she said she would get the consent form notarized and have it faxed to my prison counselor by the end of the week. A week before Mother's Day my daughter

Kadijah was approved to come visit me. On Mother's Day one of my younger sisters, Starr, flew in from Boston for a surprise visit. Starr is the one who had long ago introduced me to Neisy, and as they say, the rest is history. That weekend Starr and Neisy planned to come visit me along with Hakeem and Kadijah. This was a very special occasion for me, being that it was the first time I would meet my new daughter face-to-face. I made sure I took extra care preparing my clothes, shaving my head, and trimming up my beard.

At this time, I was being housed at Oregon State Penitentiary's minimum facility which had a large glass picture window in the exercise room through which you could see the parking lot. During visiting hours, the inmates used the exercise room as a makeshift waiting room, because the picture window allowed you to watch your visitors when they arrived.

After about twenty minutes of waiting, finally I saw Neisy's silver 1997 Lincoln Continental. Once parked, the door's opened up, and Starr got out of the front passenger side, then both back doors opened up and my son and daughter got out. Finally, the driver's door opened and a beautiful sight emerged: A petit powerhouse, the mother of my now-two children. I watched them amble through the gate and into the building. I was so excited it was hard for me to contain my smile. Once everyone was logged in by the visiting officer, my name was paged over the intercom. I was already at the inmate visiting door when they called me.

The door opened and I entered the small search room; the officer inside patted me down, logged me in, then called out "visit" and the door buzzed and I walked through. On entering the visiting room, I instantly spotted my visitors, and caught a whiff of Neisey's signature essence of rosewater scent that had always intoxicated me. But, before I made it half way to them, Kadijah charged toward me as fast as she could, giggling and calling out "Daddy!" She jumped into my arms. I picked up this soft bundle that smelled of sweet candy, this leggy little doe-eyed girl who was now my new daughter. We both looked at each other and smiled.

I kissed her on her perfect pudgy cheek and looked to Hakeem. To my surprise, he didn't look like the happy kid I knew him to be. As I walked over to him with his sister still in my arms it dawned on me that my son was always the one who would run and jump into my arms when he came to visit.

I now realized that I had a serious problem on my hands: Jealousy. For the entire visit Kadijah sat on my lap which was, again, my son's habit. For the most part, it was a great visit, but I was concerned that Hakeem's adjustment was going to be difficult. I understood how my son felt, because for the first eight years of his life he never had to compete for my attention or love. The last thing I wanted was for him to feel like I had abandoned him or traded him in.

Chapter 10: PARENTING POINTS

- If you have multiple children make sure to give an equal amount of attention to each child.

- Children are very sensitive and you must be ever so careful dealing with their emotions.

- Always express to the mother of your children that new relationships forged with any of her children will be honored and respected.

- Give your first child/children time to adjust to new additions or changes in your relationship with them.

Chapter Eleven

Making the Adjustment

A WEEK HAD PASSED SINCE I had had my first visit with Kadijah. It was my weekly call day, so I picked up the phone and dialed Neisy's number. I spoke with my children's mother first and asked her how things were going since the bittersweet visit with them. Neisy told me things were great and that every other word out Kadijah's mouth had been, my Dad this, my Dad that. I smiled when she told me that. It felt good to know I was able to make this innocent child feel loved.

Neisy said she was excited to see how Kadijah and I would mesh. I laughed and told her that little girl had a mind of her own. I could feel the positive energy flowing in our conversation which gave me a sense of peace. I talked a bit longer with Neisy then we said our good-byes and I asked her to put Kadijah on the phone. After a second or two of silence I heard my sweet little girl say excitedly, "Hi Daddy!" I asked how she was doing and how her summer was going. She said it was going well, then immediately asked when she was going to see me again. Of course, all I could say was soon. Then she told me something that was very upsetting. She said that her brother and her cousin had been teasing her, telling her that I was not her real father. I was instantly taken aback by that statement; I told her not to worry and that they were just being mean. I told her that I was her Dad no matter what anyone said.

When Kadijah and I finished talking I asked her to put her mother back on the phone. I asked Neisy if she knew our son and his cousin were teasing our daughter, taunting Kadijah that I wasn't her real father. Neisy sounded concerned and said she was unaware of this teasing. I explained how I thought Hakeem may be a little jealous because I was now his sister's Dad, too. Neisy pretty much agreed with me. I then asked her where Hakeem was and she said he was at his cousin's house. I asked her to please talk with him in the meantime until I got a chance to do so, and to really see how Hakeem actually felt about sharing me with his sister.

I spoke with my son about the decision I had made when I agreed to also take care of and love Kadijah as my own. And Hakeem was fine with that. I now know I should have pondered a lot longer and deeper how Hakeem's feelings would be affected. I didn't want my son to feel like he was being pushed out. He had had to deal with a lot of pain with me not being there for him for the last five years. I had to be able to make my daughter feel welcome without my son feeling unwelcome and unloved.

My first instincts told me that maybe I should have Hakeem and Kadijah visit me separately, but I didn't believe that this was the answer to this new problem. On one hand, I had to remember all the emotional turmoil Hakeem had been through due to me being away from him, him being physically abused by a family member, and watching his mother suffer through a physically abusive relationship. So, I knew I had to be very careful dealing with my son's feelings. He needed my strength and support as his father but most of all, the assurance I had provided for him. On the other hand, Kadijah had now had an empty void in her life filled with me taking on the role of her father.

But she had also watched her mother suffer through an abusive relationship, and I, being a positive male figure in her life, was also very important. My daughter's emotional state was also very fragile just as her biological father had been missing from her life for the last five years also. So, my presence was insurance to her having a healthy childhood. It was crucial that I be allowed to give my son and daughter the support they needed without making either of them feel neglected. More so my son, helping him to adjust to this new situation was very critical, because at this moment in time I was serving all of my daughter's paternity needs. The last thing I wanted was for my son to feel like he was losing his father.

How do you explain to a child who has already felt the loss of a parent due to incarceration that you will still be there for them, even though you are dividing their time in half to share with another child?

Incarcerated fathers including me, never get enough time to spend with our children during visits, which may range from two to three hours depending on the institution. For most prisoners seeing their child or children twice a month is pretty good, compared to inmates who never get to see their children at all. During my first three years, I was only able to see my son once a month, but once I was moved closer to Portland where my son was living, I was able to see him at least twice a month. Even with an extra visit a month we were still a million miles away from a normal relationship between a son and a father. Even though he was happy when we visited, I still saw a certain sadness in his composure.

During my second visit with Hakeem and Kadijah, Hakeem became very emotional during the visit, crying about every little thing I asked him to do. He even went into his bad attitude mode and didn't want to partake in any of the games we were playing. After the visit was over I was very concerned with Hakeem's behavior, so later that evening I called to talk with him to see how he was feeling. First, I spoke with Neisy about his behavior and how neither of us had ever witnessed him act that way during any of the previous visits. She then told me that my son asked if Kadijah had to come on the next visit. When Neisy asked him why, he said that he didn't want his sister to come because she sat on my lap the whole time and hogged up the visit.

We talked a little more about Hakeem's behavior, and then I asked her to put him on the phone. When he got on the phone I asked him if he was feeling better. He said he was and then apologized for the way he was acting during our visit; I think his mother put him up to that. I told him I wasn't upset and that I was proud of him for sharing his Dad with his sister. I explained to Hakeem how Kadijah also needs a Dad to love her like I love him and that he is being a great big brother.

I reinforced to Hakeem that Kadijah was not taking his place and no one ever will. I then told him the special place he holds by being my firstborn son. My son, being the smart-aleck that he is, replied, "But I'm your only son." This made me laugh and I responded, "I know that."

After Hakeem and I finished talking, I decided that a few

individual visits with my son and daughter were a good idea. I gave my mother a call and told her about the visit I had had with my son and daughter and the statements my son had made about his sister sitting on my lap the whole time during our first visit together and in his opinion hogging up all the visiting time. I told her about my idea of a few separate visits to help Hakeem adjust. My mother agreed this was probably a good idea. She said she would bring Hakeem up to see me the next week; this way I wouldn't have their mother trying to choose whom to bring and whom to leave. This way no one would feel left out.

My only concern was Hakeem going back bragging to his sister about coming to visit me. You know how kids are, especially when they feel like they are in competition with each other. I didn't want to seem one-sided on this subject, just as I was concerned with my son making a positive transition with me being Kadijah's father, I was also concerned with my daughter making a positive transition to me being her father. This is a responsibility that I took on for the rest of my life and hers as well. It was important that we started on the right foot and that she trusted and respected me. She had already had to experience life for four years without a father after having watched her mother endure years of abuse from yet another man she feared and for whom she had no respect. My role in Kadijah's life had to be completely positive and loving.

So, for the moment, my daughter had gone from four years of having no positive male figure in her life, to having her mother's new boyfriend who was a complete picture of negativity, whom Kadijah had to watch mistreat her mother. That's really why I feel she and I connected in the first place, and bonded so quickly and easily. She saw the positivity and love I gave my son. And truthfully, what child doesn't want that? I know of no child in this world who doesn't need two parents to love them, nurture them, protect them, and teach them how to survive in this world.

I guess for now I would have to take very carefully and slowly this new role I was playing in both my children's lives. Both their emotional states were very fragile and they had endured unnecessary stress throughout their short-lived existences. As their father, it was my duty to protect them even if it was from each other's own need to feel loved by Dad.

In time, I knew that everything would work out, but the key word here is time and also being very receptive to children's emotions. Children constantly show their parent in different ways when something is bothering them. Sadly, we as parents are sometimes too busy or engulfed in other life crises that take our attention away from our children. This is why I believe it is so important to give your children as much of your time as possible. And when you've done that, find more time to give them. In this society, we live in today we have learned to let other people and devices parent our children.

We are quick to tell our children to go watch TV or go play outside or drop them off at some after school program, or the home of a family member or friend when we are supposedly too busy to deal with them. The more you are in tune with your children the better you'll be able to parent them. But more importantly, you'll be able to help prepare them to deal with problems that are sure to arise in their lives.

Chapter 11: PARENTING POINTS

- With multiple children, parse your visit to ensure time for an individual visit with each child.
- Regardless if you're free or incarcerated spend as much time with your children as possible.
- Be aware that changes in your normal routine may affect your child's or children's emotional state.
- Develop a personal relationship with each of your children.

Chapter Twelve

Putting Our Children First

AS MEN, WHY DO WE think that making babies and not providing for them is acceptable? Is it because many of us were abandoned by our own fathers when we ourselves were children? This may be the case, but it's not an excuse to continue that same cowardly pattern. If you don't want to take the responsible path of raising your child or children then you should have protected sex or refrain from sex altogether. Frankly, it is unacceptable to shrug off the fact that you brought a child into this world, and then decided you don't feel like doing your duty supporting that child emotionally, physically, and financially.

Neglecting your duties as a parent and giving no contribution to your child's life and future, should be considered a form of child abuse. It's like starving your child. How long would your child be able to survive without necessary nourishment? Abandoning your children is the same as not feeding them. How can they live a healthy life without a parent's love and nourishment? Some will survive, but how many have perished because a father or mother decided to put reckless impulses first? How can we prepare our children to be the leaders of the future when we leave them to be directed by poverty, drugs, gangs, sexual predators, and ignorant minds?

Fathers are one of four cornerstones for a child's healthy growth and positive skill building—the other three cornerstones are the child's mother, the community into which you bring your child, and the child's education. The father must show them strength, leadership, responsibility, and sacrifice. Without fathers how can there be a future? Fathers give their son's and daughter's the skills to raise their own future families. For the son, the father teaches him how to be a man, and what it means to be a man. He also teaches his son the necessary steps to be the foundation and backbone of his future family.

Through his example, a father teaches his son how to be responsible, how to be a leader, gives him a work ethic, and the essential skills required to survive in this world. For a daughter, a father teaches her to lead responsibly and be strong as an individual, and as a woman when dealing with a man in a relationship, how to expect respect. The father is the daughter's mold in which to cast her future husband. If the father is a good example, taking care of all his responsibilities, honoring his wife, supporting his family, and leading them to success, his daughter won't settle for a man with lesser qualities and characteristics.

Why are there so many single-family homes in America today? The majority of them are being maintained by the mother, which leaves the young sons of America to grow up with incomplete knowledge of how to be a man. So, if a boy grows up without his father and is never taught how to be a man, then he cannot pass down this jewel to his future son. Eventually the future generations of men will become extinct and all that will be left is a bunch of large boys. With this cycle continuing over a period of time the knowledge of being a responsible man altogether will become extinct, because there will be no knowing person remaining to pass down the knowledge and skill that it takes to produce responsible men. Moms do a great job, but they cannot know viscerally, intimately, what men experience as they fledge from boyhood to manhood.

Where do we start to ensure that we survive as a species of Homo sapien males? Who is accountable? I believe we must first recognize the problem, because before you can cure yourself, you have to know that you are sick. Once you recognize that you are sick, you can then find the proper remedy. The first step to curing this sickness of fathers missing from their children's lives is for fathers to hold themselves accountable. A lot of us as males grew up without much responsibility.

If we grew up as an only child with our mother being the only parent, it's more than likely she cushioned us, buffering aches and pains that came along with learning to be responsible. If you grew up in a family as a male, and the other siblings were young women, they were the ones who were ususlly taught how to cook, clean, wash, sew, and raise children. We as males in the family usually had responsibilities like taking out the trash, sweeping the floor, or doing yard work. But rarely are we given the basic survival tools our sisters are taught. This in turn leaves most of us males inadequate as individual men even to cook, clean, or wash our own clothes— essentials everyone should know how to do, male or female.

Most of us men feel that as long as we are able to get money then we are doing well, but there's more to life than just financial gain. Some men make the mistake of believing that doing whatever it takes to make money makes you a man. Sad to say, there are countless men who can testify that this shortsighted and narrow-minded thinking only leads to prison or death. As I have said, we must first hold ourselves accountable as men, then as fathers, and step up to the plate to accept the role of responsible leaders, role models, teachers, providers, and protectors—this is what makes a man a man!

Secondly, we must stay actively involved in our children's lives. If we as fathers are not on good terms with the mother of our children, we should try, and take the time to find a way to mend old wounds. At least to the point whereby both parents have a clear understanding that the child needs them both. With both parents involved in a child's life, the odds of that child becoming successful greatly improve. But with just one parent raising a child, s/he is automatically reduced to a 50% chance of being successful. If you are still holding feelings for the mother of your children, but you're upset because you can't be with her, then man up and put your feelings aside, and put the feelings and needs of your child first, especially if you have been using your emotions, self-pity, and anger as a crutch to not stay active in your child's life!

If drugs or alcohol are playing a part in your absence from your child's life, then you must make a choice and ask yourself if getting high is more important than being there for your child. Is it not our duty to warn and guide our children away from the mistakes we've made? If we are using the excuse that no one taught you how to be a father, then now is the time to learn! Google it! Or, go to the library and find books on parenting. Talk to older, responsible men in your community. It's your job as a parent to do whatever it takes to learn and acquire the knowledge needed to raise your children and mold them into responsible adults.

We must stop being selfish, putting our own wants for enjoyment and pleasure before our children's basic needs which—I underscore again—are your child's birthright. It's pretty simple: If you cannot find a responsible person to watch your child then you cannot go out to the club. Sit your butt down and read to your child, and when s/he sleeps for the night, sit your butt down again and plan what you're going to do for your child tomorrow and the next day and the day after that. We must prioritize, what's more important: Going out to party for a few hours or making sure your children are safe and the environment is safe for them to dwell in?

Even using the mentality of, I'll just party at home can be damaging to a child, especially when you're partaking in activities that are non-conducive to your child's safety and health. How do you expect your children to stay away from drugs and alcohol when they are watching a parent consume these poisons? For too long, parents have used the platitude, "Do as I say, not as I do", which is just another way to dodge responsibility and accountability.

In order for anything to grow—whether plants or human beings—you must first invest in the proper environment for them to grow in, then you must provide time, care, and attention to ensure healthy growth. It's essential for us as fathers to make time for our children. No amount of money, fame, recognition, or admiration from peers or the world is more important than making time for your children. So many of us as fathers are caught up in the right now instead of planning for the future. Too long have we fed our children to the beast known as failure. How can we expect our children to succeed if we don't teach them how to succeed? I can truly say that I don't ever want my children to make the mistakes I made. It would be selfish of me not to explain verbally and visually the bad choices I made to my children.

Every decision you make will in some way affect your children, whether directly or indirectly. My father may not have always been there for me, but he was never hard for me to find. That alone made a difference in my life. A mother can only teach her son so much, and even though she is a role model for her son and daughter she cannot teach what it is to be a man. Biological distinctions aside, as fathers, we have to be careful how our sons see us treating women. We must teach our sons, and our daughters, to respect women and honor them. For our daughters we have to teach them that they are to be respected and cherished. This will enable them to set the standard for any man who wishes to form an intimate relationship with them.

Society has made it acceptable to objectify women, and we as fathers have to teach our daughters to never sacrifice their dignity to gain a man's love and attention. We must also put sharp emphasis on our children's education, volunteer to partake in school field trips, and other school related functions and activities. Help your children study for upcoming tests and check their homework regularly. Take time to meet their teachers, because apart from you, their teachers spend the majority of each day with your children. Teachers, too, are a good source of information about what's going on in your children's lives.

Things that we may see as not really important, like eating

dinner with our children, can have a great deal of impact on their future and the way they interact with others. The dinner table is a place where the family is able to come together as a whole, which gives parents and children quality time to interact with one another.

This is also a good way to monitor your children's daily activities and find out if they are having problems in a particular area of their lives. It's also a good time to tell your children how you're doing. You may not know this but your children can sense when you are under pressure or stressed, and stress has the ability to become infectious. The dinner table is a great place to talk about current events in the community and around the world, and how these events may be affecting the way we currently live and how our future may change for the better or not, due to the outcome of current events. Dinner time is also good for discussing other topics you feel are relevant to your children's success and future.

Due to work schedules and a lot of homes being run by one parent, children are getting less one-on-one time with parents. For instance, if you are a father and you have visitation with your children for the weekends (or however your situation is arranged), your time is limited with them. In a lot of situations like these, the non-custodial parent will just try to make sure their children are pacified by doing all the fun things kid's love to do. Use some of that time that you have with them to find out what's going on in their lives. A lot of times when parents separate or divorce, the non-custodial parent will try to erase the fact that they are no longer a family by using material items, with the hope to reform the bond and erase any feelings of pain, resentment, anger, and abandonment.

This can be very dangerous because not only are you teaching them to hide and suppress their feelings, but you are also giving them the notion that material things can buy love and affection. No one is perfect. We all make mistakes in our lives and may continue to make mistakes. But the biggest mistake we can make is not being a part of our children's life. To not love and cherish them due to our own misled wants and desires is unacceptable, plain and simple. If you don't want the responsibility of children, I have two—and only two—words for you:

Use protection!

Condoms and birth control are available at any neighborhood

corner store. Think about the life you would be squandering by not being responsible. The Creator gave children two parents for a reason, to care for them and teach them until they are old enough to teach and care for themselves. Be there for your children and you'll have done your duty as a father and as a human being.

It's not really that hard.

And it's fun.

All you have to do is be there.

Show up.

Man up.

Be a Dad!

Chapter 12: PARENTING POINTS

- Put your children's needs before your own wants and needs.
- Do not use drugs or alcohol as an excuse to not provide for your children.
- Always provide a safe environment for your children.
- Be a role model for your children—you're the adult in the equation.

Forgiving

Admirable

Thoughtful

Headstrong

Efficient

Rational

About the Author

Latif Bossman is a writer due to circumstance. Sentenced to 70 months in prison in 2001 with no options for parole, he was faced with the dilemma of parenting behind bars. With 24 months remaining on his sentence, he decided to write about his experience as a father behind bars.

As a writer, Prison Fathers: Parenting Behind Bars is his first work. Latif is also working on a curriculum for a parenting program for men incarcerated called P.O.P., which stands for Parenting Over Prison. Latif is a father of four and lives in Portland, Oregon.

Experienced writing hip hop music for more than 20 years, writing Prison Fathers: Parenting Behind Bars came naturally to Latif. Using various methods and new techniques he developed while in prison, he was able to continue to have a positive relationship with his children until his release.

Latif completed a certification course on the Essentials of Communication and Collaboration from Rockford University.

In 2017, Latif completed his manuscript Prison Fathers: Parenting Behind Bars. From 2011 to 2015 he served as a board member for the International Center for Traditional Childbearing. Latif also served as a panelist in 2012 with two appearances on the internet talk show Ghetto Rise Media. In 2001 as a member of the rap group P-Style Latif and group member Keary Kase released their first hip hop single "Life of A Star," which won the Battle of the Beats contest on radio station 95.5 which was hosted by basketball super star Rasheed Wallace (then a member of the Portland Trail Blazers, at the time the song was aired.